Ready for PET

coursebook

Nick Kenny
Anne Kelly

Macmillan Education
4 Crinan Street
London N1 9XW
A division of Macmillan Publishers Limited
Companies and representatives throughout the world

ISBN 978-0-230-02072-6 (without Key)
ISBN 978-0-230-01030-7 (with Key)

First published 2001
This edition 2007

Designed by Jim Evoy
Illustrated by Mike Atkinson; John Dillow; Peter Harper; Janos Jantner; Ken Harvey; Martin Sanders; David Smith
Cover design by Andrew Oliver

The authors would like to thank Barbara Lewis, David Foll, Penny Beck, Margaret van Doelen, Nelson Aurich, Graciela Mazzucco and Russell Crew-Gee for their help with this book.

The publishers would like to thank the following consultants and teachers for piloting and reviewing this book: Andy Hannaford, Anthony Matthews, Barbara Lewis, Gail Butler, Mabel Turner and Sarah Ellis.

The authors and publishers would like to thank the following for permission to reproduce copyright material: University of Cambridge Local Examinations Syndicate for the answer sheets on pp.92–3.
Extract from 'What it fees like… to win an Oscar' by Adam Jacques copyright © The Independent/Adam Jacques 2006, first published in The Independent on Sunday 26.02.06, reprinted by permission of the publisher. Extract from 'The Cooking Bus goes round and round' by Tom Moggach copyright © Guardian Newspapers Limited 2006, first published in the Guardian 07.02.06, reprinted by permission of the publisher. Extract from 'Days Out: Dinosaur Isle and Fossil Walk, Isle of Wight' by Juliet Rix copyright © The Independent/Juliet Rix 2006, first published in The Independent on Sunday 23.04.06, reprinted by permission of the publisher. Extract from 'Living in a house felt like prison' by Ros Anderson copyright © Guardian Newspapers Limited 2006, first published in The Guardian 15.04.06, reprinted by permission of the publisher. Extract from 'Heaven on the high seas' by Jenny Cockle copyright © The Independent/Jenny Cockle 2006, first published in The Independent on Sunday 19.02.06, reprinted by permission of the publisher. Extract from 'What it feels like… to balloon around the world non-stop' by Richard Middleton copyright © The Independent/Richard Middleton 2006, first published in The Independent on Sunday 28.05.06, reprinted by permission of the publisher. Extract from 'The man who makes children fly' by Maria Harding copyright © The Telegraph 2006, first published in The Daily Telegraph 26.04.06, reprinted by permission of the publisher. Extract from 'To the ends of the earth' by Jenny Cockle copyright © The Independent/Jenny Cockle 2006, first published in The Independent on Sunday 07.05.06, reprinted by permission of the publisher.

The authors and publishers would like to thank the following for permission to reproduce their photographic material: Alamy/ Andrew Holt p31(t), Alamy/Adrianko p60; BananaStock p41(a); Brand X Pictures p49; Corbis/Royalty Free pp19(t), 57(l), Corbis/David Giles p25(A), Corbis/Michael Dunn p25(B), Corbis/ Stephanie Colasanti p51; Empics/William Conran/ PA p31(b); Eye Ubiquitous/Craig Hutchins pp39(A & B), 48(A), Eye Ubiquitous/Tim Hawkins p48(B), Eye Ubiquitous/Julia Waterlow p48(C); FLPA/Fred Bavendam p19(l), FLPA/David Hosking p19(cl), Funday Times p44; Getty Images/Taxi pp12(A & B), 27, 38, 63(B), Getty/Stone pp33, 42, 47(B), Getty/Loren Santow p43; Haddon Davies p54; Image Source p57(r); MHELT pp16(1–5), 28, MHELT/Chris Honeywell p18(A), MHELT/Sue Baker p18(B); NHPA/Kevin Schafer p19(r); Pathfinder p76(t); PhotoAlto p76(r); Photodisc pp61, 47(A) Photolibrary/Tui de Roy p19(cr); Stockbyte pp63(A), 87; SuperStock/age footstock p6(r), SuperStock/Royalty Free p41(b).

Cover and title page photos
©Thinkstock (ml), ©Digital Vision (l, mr), ©Photodisk (r)

Printed and bound in Thailand

2017 2016 2015
15 14 13 12

With Answer Key

2016 2015 2014
15 14 13 12

Contents

Introduction

Ready for PET is for students of English who are preparing to take the University of Cambridge Preliminary English Test (PET). *Ready for PET* will get you ready for this test in three important ways. First, it will give you practice in doing the kinds of exercises you will do in the test. Then, it will give you advice on how you can do your best in these exercises. Finally, it will help you learn the vocabulary you need to do the writing and speaking exercises fluently. In this way, you can feel confident about your English when you do the test.

You can use *Ready for PET* in your English class with your teacher, or you can use it to get ready for the test by yourself.

What is the Preliminary English Test (PET)?

The University of Cambridge has tests for students of English at five different levels, from beginners to very advanced students.

PET is at level 2 and is for lower intermediate students. PET tests your reading, writing, listening and speaking. You get 25% of the total marks for the test for each of these four skills. There are three different papers.

Paper 1 is Reading and Writing and takes 1 hour and 30 minutes. In this paper, there are five reading parts and three writing parts. In the reading part of the paper, you have to read some texts and answer some questions on each one. For these questions, you answer by choosing A, B, C or D. In the writing part of the paper, you have to do a short grammar exercise, write a short message, and then write a letter or story. This is a summary of the Reading and Writing paper:

Paper 1: Reading and Writing (1 hour 30 minutes)			
	Type of text	**Type of question**	**Number of questions and marks**
Reading			
Part 1	five signs, notices or messages	reading comprehension: multiple choice	5
Part 2	eight short texts	reading comprehension: matching	5
Part 3	one text	reading comprehension: correct/not correct	10
Part 4	one text	reading comprehension: multiple choice	5
Part 5	one text	vocabulary and grammar: multiple choice	10
Writing			
Part 1		grammar	5
Part 2		writing a short message	1 question: 5 marks
Part 3		writing a letter or story	1 question: 15 marks

Paper 2 is Listening and takes about 30 minutes. There are four parts to the paper. You have to listen to a recording and answer some questions. For the questions for three parts, you answer by choosing A, B or C and for one part you write down a few words or numbers. You hear each part of the recording twice. This is a summary of the Listening paper:

Paper 2: Listening (approximately 30 minutes)			
	Type of text	Type of question	Number of questions and marks
Part 1	seven short recordings (one or two people speaking)	multiple choice pictures	7
Part 2	one or two people speaking	multiple choice	6
Part 3	one person speaking	writing down words	6
Part 4	two people speaking	correct/not correct	6

Paper 3 is Speaking and takes 10–12 minutes. There are four parts to the paper. You do the Speaking test with another student. In the Speaking test, you and your partner talk to an examiner and to each other, while another examiner listens to you. The examiner will ask you some questions and give you some instructions about what you should talk about. In two parts, you have some pictures to talk about. This is a summary of the Speaking paper:

Paper 3: Speaking (10–12 minutes)	
Part 1	The examiner asks you and your partner questions about yourselves.
Part 2	You and your partner look at some pictures showing a situation and talk about it together.
Part 3	You and your partner take it in turns to describe a photograph each.
Part 4	You and your partner have a conversation about the subject (eg holidays) of your photos.

You will find more detailed information about each part of all three papers in the different lessons of *Ready for PET.*

How *Ready for PET* is organized

There are ten units in *Ready for PET* and each unit has two lessons. In each unit, you will find exercises to practise the reading, writing, listening and speaking skills, and the vocabulary and grammar you will need in PET. In each lesson of Units 1–8 there is detailed information and advice about one particular part of the test, and in Units 9–10 you can revise all the advice that has gone before. Throughout the book there are **Get ready** boxes containing clear, helpful exam tips.

At the end of the book there are two PET practice tests. When you do these, you will experience what it is like taking the real test. You will see how much time you have to do each question and you will find out which parts of the test you need to practise more.

The **CD-ROM** which comes with the book has six Reading, Writing and Listening tests. These tests provide extensive practice of PET test tasks.

When you've worked through *Ready for PET*, you'll know what to expect in every part of the test, and you'll have the language you need to do the test well.

For students studying alone

If you are preparing for PET without a teacher, *Ready for PET* will help you. You should use *Ready for PET* at the same time as your general English coursebook. Your coursebook will develop your knowledge of English, and *Ready for PET* will give you the special practice you need for the test exercises.

Remember to use the 'with key' edition of *Ready for PET,* which has a key to exercises and recording scripts of the listening texts at the back. When you have finished each exercise, check your answers with the key. Don't look at the key until you have done each exercise. If necessary, you can use a dictionary to help you with unknown words, but always try to guess the meaning of words first. You should also see if you can answer the questions without knowing the difficult words.

The texts of the listening exercises are on a CD. In the PET Listening test, you hear each listening text twice, so when you are practising with these exercises, listen twice before checking your answers. If you don't understand something you can look at the recording script, but never do this until you have listened to the recording twice.

There are many writing exercises in *Ready for PET*. It's useful if you can ask a teacher to correct these for you, but it doesn't matter if this isn't possible. Just doing the writing is good practice. Always make sure you follow the instructions exactly and check your own work carefully.

There are also many speaking exercises in the book. It's difficult to do speaking exercises if you're studying alone, but it's important that you get speaking practice. Remember, 25% of the marks for the whole of PET are for the Speaking test, so if possible, do the speaking exercises with another student. If you can't do this, do the exercises by yourself and record what you say. Then listen to yourself speaking and think of ways in which you could do the exercise better. Don't worry about making mistakes, but try to express your ideas clearly.

On pages 66–87, there are two practice tests. You should try to do at least one of these like a real test. Only take the amount of time allowed for the test, and do it without any dictionary or notes to help you.

You can also use the CD-ROM to give yourself practice doing PET Reading, Writing and Listening tasks. There are six tests on the CD-ROM. Do a test at regular intervals while you are studying. Check your answers and keep a record of your scores to get an idea of the progress you are making.

Before you start, decide how many hours a week you can spend studying with *Ready for PET* and keep to this decision. It is better to study regularly for short periods than to try and do everything just before the day of the test.

The PET preparation diary on the opposite page will help you to organize your study. Fill in the date you start your PET preparation at the top, and the date you will take PET at the bottom. Then work out how many days or weeks you have to complete each unit of this book. When you have completed a unit, write the date in the space provided, and decide how well you have done in the different practice exercises in that unit (self-assessment). In the 'Study notes' section you can write anything which will help you. For example, you may want to make a note of some exercises you want to look at again, or some exercises which you haven't had time to do and plan to work on later. You can also keep a record of the scores you get on the CD-ROM Practice tests. You should organize your study in the way which best suits you in the time you have available before you take PET.

PET preparation diary

I began preparing for PET on: (date) ....

Unit	Study notes	Self-assessment ✔ = I did well ✘ = I need more practice	CD-ROM Practice tests
1 completed on		Reading Listening Speaking Writing Vocabulary	**Practice test 1** Date .... Total Reading score .... Total Listening score ....
2 completed on		Reading Listening Speaking Writing Vocabulary	
3 completed on		Reading Listening Speaking Writing Vocabulary	**Practice test 2** Date .... Total Reading score .... Total Listening score ....
4 completed on		Reading Listening Speaking Writing Vocabulary	**Practice test 3** Date .... Total Reading score .... Total Listening score ....
5 completed on		Reading Listening Speaking Writing Vocabulary	
6 completed on		Reading Listening Speaking Writing Vocabulary	**Practice test 4** Date .... Total Reading score .... Total Listening score ....
7 completed on		Reading Listening Speaking Writing Vocabulary	
8 completed on		Reading Listening Speaking Writing Vocabulary	**Practice test 5** Date .... Total Reading score .... Total Listening score ....
9 completed on		Reading Speaking Writing Vocabulary	
10 completed on		Reading Listening Speaking Writing Vocabulary	**Practice test 6** Date .... Total Reading score .... Total Listening score ....

I am taking PET on: (test date) ....

1 1

Personal information

1 Writing

Complete this form with information about yourself.

SIGN UP NOW!

Name:

Surname:

Home town:

E-mail address:

Mobile number:

Sex: Age:

Interests:

2 Listening 1.1

1 **Listen to two people talking about themselves and fill in the missing information.**

SIGN UP NOW!

Name:

Surname:

Home town:

E-mail address:

Mobile number:

Sex: Age:

Interests:

A

SIGN UP NOW!

Name:

Surname:

Home town:

E-mail address:

Mobile number:

Sex: Age:

Interests:

B

2 **If you wanted to find out more information about these people, what questions would you ask? Make questions beginning with each of these words.**

What ... ?

Are ... ?

Where ... ?

Do ... ?

When ... ?

How ... ?

3 Speaking

1 **Look at the activities in the box. Which of these activities are you good at? Order the activities from most interesting (1) to least interesting (12).**

Talk about why you like (1) and why you dislike (12).

watching sports	playing sports	computer games
watersports	collecting things	playing a musical instrument
dancing	learning languages	making things
driving	keep-fit exercises	surfing the Internet

2 **How do you spell your name? Practise saying the letters in English.**

1.2 3 **Listen to five people spelling their names. Write their names below:**

1 ……………….. **2** ……………….. **3** ………………..
4 ……………….. **5** ………………..

Talk to the examiner.
Answer the questions!
Make your answers interesting!

Get ready for PET Speaking Part 1

1 In Part 1 of the Speaking Test, the examiner asks you questions. Be ready to talk about:
- your home and family
- what you do every day
- your work and studies
- your likes and dislikes

2 When you answer, remember to:
- say what you really think
- answer the questions directly
- say why – give reasons and examples
- make the conversation interesting
- talk to the examiner, not to your partner

3 The examiner also asks you to spell your name.
- Practise spelling all parts of your name.
- Make sure you can do it perfectly.
- Make sure you can do it at normal speed.

4 Writing

Complete the second sentence so that it means the same as the first, using no more than three words.

1 Do you play football well?
Are you a ……………………… player?
2 Do watersports interest you?
Are you ……………………… watersports?
3 What is your age?
How ……………………… you?
4 Which is your favourite school subject?
Which school subject ……………………… like best?
5 How is your surname spelt?
How do ……………………… your surname?

5 Writing

You have decided to join an English-language club on the Internet. Write a brief description of yourself for the database. You can write up to 100 words. Remember to include:

- your personal details, for example, name and age
- what you do/study
- the things that you are interested in

6 Listening

1 **David and Victoria have just met at a party. Complete the gaps in their conversation using the phrases below. Write the correct letters in the spaces.**

David: Hello. I'm David.
Victoria: **(1)** ....
David: Yes, I'm one of his friends too, and we play football together. What do you study?
Victoria: **(2)** ....
David: I've finished college, actually, and I'm working as a windsurfing instructor.
Victoria: **(3)** ....
David: That doesn't matter. You could learn.
Victoria: **(4)** ....
David: So am I. I'm running a course which starts next week. Would you be interested in joining?
Victoria: **(5)** ....

Use five of these phrases to complete Victoria's part of the conversation.

A English. Have you finished college?
B Yes, I suppose so. But what I'm really interested in is sailing.
C Hi. I'm Victoria. I'm a friend of Tom's from college.
D Hello, I'm Victoria. I'm really interested in football.
E I'm doing languages. What about you?
F Oh, I'm really interested in watersports, but I'm not very good at windsurfing.
G Oh … I might be … it depends.

1.3 2 **Which two didn't you use? Now listen and check.**

3 **When you meet someone of your own age for the first time:**

- what questions do you ask them?
- what are good things to talk about?
- what do you tell them about yourself?

7 Reading

1 **Look at these notices and choose the correct explanation, A, B or C.**

This notice is telling you

A what information to write.
B which type of letters to use.
C which type of pen to use.

1

Please write in
BLOCK CAPITALS

This notice is giving you

A some advice.
B a suggestion.
C an instruction.

2

ALL PACKAGES
MUST BE
SIGNED FOR

2 **What is a signature? How is it different from other ways of writing your name?**
Write your name in block capitals: ....
Write your signature: ....

1 2 A regular thing

1 Vocabulary

1 **Match the words in A with the words in B. For example, *comb* and *hair* go together. Some words are used more than once.**

A

attend	boil	brush	clean	comb
dial	dust	feed	iron	miss
tidy	tie	wash		

B

bus	class	desk	dishes
furniture	hair	meeting	number
pet	shirt	shoes	
shoelaces	teeth	water	

Which of these things do you do regularly, sometimes, occasionally or never? Talk about some of your habits using the words in the boxes.

2 **Now match the words in C with the words in D. Some words are used more than once.**

C

hand in	join in	take off
put on	put up	put away
turn up	plug in	turn on

D

books	game	homework
make-up	music	radio
socks	umbrella	light

Use the words in the boxes to talk about your daily life.

2 Reading

What kinds of short message do you write to people in your daily life? Read these short messages.

A

Mum,
All my white sports shirts are dirty! I must wear a clean one in the tennis match tomorrow. Could you wash and iron one for me? If you can, I'll wash up after dinner every night for a week! Thanks a lot.
Julia

B

E-mail:

To: Paulo
From: Emilio

Thanks for telling me about the English homework. I'm worried I won't be able to do it because I missed the lesson. Why don't you come to my house on Saturday and we can do the exercises together?

C

POSTCA

Dear Gemma,
My cousin Lou and I visited Brighton yesterday. What a pity you couldn't come with us! We went shopping, and then we visited a beautiful old palace called Brighton Pavilion. My favourite part of the day was eating ice cream on the beach.
Love, Jodie

In which message (or messages), is the writer

1 thanking someone for something?
2 describing what s/he has done?
3 explaining why s/he needs to have something?
4 telling someone what s/he liked best about something?
5 asking someone to do something for him/her?
6 saying how s/he feels about something?
7 suggesting an activity?
8 offering to do something?

3 Writing

1 **Imagine this situation and then write a short message to a classmate.**
You want to ask a classmate to help you do something.
Write a note to your classmate. In your note, you should

- explain what help you'd like your classmate to give you
- suggest a time when your classmate can help you
- offer to do something for your classmate

Write 35–45 words.

2 **Read your classmate's note to you and then write another note in reply.**
In your note, you should

- agree to help your classmate
- suggest a *different* time to give this help
- accept your classmate's offer

Remember to write something about each point – that's three things to write.

Write 35–45 words.

Get ready for PET Writing Part 2

1 The first line of the instructions describes a situation to you. Read this carefully and imagine the situation.
2 The instructions tell you to write *three* points in your message. Make sure you say something about each point.
3 Remember to address your message to the person named in the instructions (eg *Dear Alice, Hi Ben*).
4 Don't forget to write your name at the end of your message.
5 Don't write fewer than 35 words or more than 45 words.
6 Check what you have written.

3 **Write one of these short messages.**
Your English friend, Alice, helped you with your English homework last week.
Write a card to send to Alice. In your card, you should

- thank Alice
- tell her what your teacher said about your homework
- suggest when you could see Alice again

Remember to write 'Dear Alice' and to sign your card.

Write 35–45 words.

You took a phone call for your English friend, Ben, about a parcel.
Write the phone message for Ben. In your message, you should

- tell Ben who phoned
- say what is in the parcel
- explain what Ben should do when the parcel arrives

Remember to check what you have written.

Write 35–45 words.

4 Writing

There are several ways to make comparisons.
Examples:

Sam listens to the radio ***more*** *often* ***than*** *Marcia does.*
Marcia listens to the radio ***less*** *often* ***than*** *Sam does.*
Marcia doesn't listen to the radio ***as*** *often* ***as*** *Sam does.*

*My shoes are clean****er than*** *my brother's.*
*My brother's shoes are dirt****ier than*** *mine.*
My brother's shoes aren't ***as*** *clean* ***as*** *mine.*

My grandmother is ***better*** *at ironing* ***than*** *my mother.*
My mother is not ***as*** *good at ironing* ***as*** *my grandmother.*
My mother is ***worse*** *at ironing* ***than*** *my grandmother.*

Complete the second sentence so that it means the same as the first, using no more than three words.

1 Your bedroom is tidier than mine.
My bedroom isn't .... yours.
2 Gerry doesn't do the washing-up as fast as Paul.
Paul does the washing-up .... Gerry.
3 The new armchair isn't nearly as comfortable as the old one.
The old armchair is much .... the new one.
4 Every evening, Sally does a lot more homework than Rachel.
Every evening, Rachel does a lot .... Sally.
5 This music isn't nearly as bad as the music they play on Radio 2.
The music they play on Radio 2 is far .... this music.

5 Reading

1 **What inventions of the last 2,000 years have caused the most important changes in people's daily lives?**

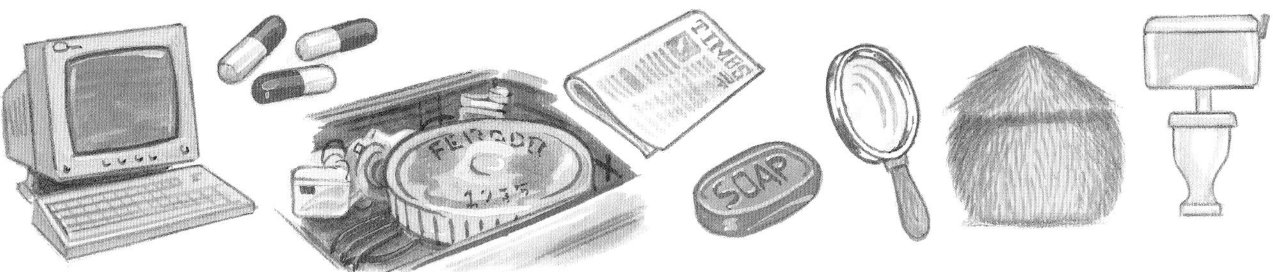

2 **Read this text and choose the correct word, A, B, C or D for each space.**

INVENTIONS OF THE LAST 2,000 YEARS

Recently, hundreds of scientists and philosophers were asked to name the most important invention of the last 2,000 years. You might **(1)** .... people to say the Internet, penicillin or the internal combustion engine, but in **(2)** .... nobody did. One scientist **(3)** .... for paper because, long before the Internet, paper allowed ideas to be sent around the world. **(4)** .... scientists agreed that modern medicine has helped millions of people, but said **(5)** .... inventions, such as soap and pipes for clean and dirty water, have **(6)** .... more lives. One philosopher said hay was the most important because it's winter food for horses. Without **(7)** ...., horses couldn't exist in cold climates, **(8)** .... meant that there couldn't be cities in places colder than Athens and Rome. So, thanks **(9)** .... hay, Vienna, Paris, London and Berlin were built! Someone else named the mirror because in **(10)** .... at our own faces we can learn about human beings in general.

1	**A** expect	**B** think	**C** believe	**D** guess
2	**A** all	**B** fact	**C** particular	**D** detail
3	**A** suggested	**B** judged	**C** answered	**D** voted
4	**A** Other	**B** Another	**C** Others	**D** Any
5	**A** clearer	**B** plainer	**C** simpler	**D** purer
6	**A** rescued	**B** delivered	**C** saved	**D** recovered
7	**A** them	**B** it	**C** these	**D** many
8	**A** what	**B** that	**C** where	**D** which
9	**A** to	**B** of	**C** by	**D** from
10	**A** seeing	**B** looking	**C** watching	**D** studying

2 1 You live and learn

1 Vocabulary

1 **Look at the photographs.**

A

B

In which of the photos can you see these things?

mouse	screen	desk
blackboard	keyboard	pen
chair	map	

somebody …	asking	thinking
	talking	reading
	explaining	waiting

2 **What other things can you see in the photographs?**

2 Speaking

1 **Look at these ideas. Which five do you think are the best ways to learn English?**

?

surfing the Internet
studying a textbook
going to classes
playing computer games
doing grammar exercises
listening to songs
watching satellite TV
talking to people in English
watching films in English
reading newspapers and magazines

1.4 2 **Listen to Polly. She is studying Spanish.**

- Which is her favourite way of studying Spanish?
- Choose the correct picture.

A ☐

B ☐

C ☐

- Why does Polly like studying in this way?

3 **You want to ask Polly about the things in the box below. Write the questions.**

the teacher	length of each class	number of students
the book(s) and equipment	type of people	cost of course
the classroom	number of classes per week	what she's learnt

3 Speaking

1 **Look at this situation.**
A young friend of yours wants to learn a new language in his free time.
He has a small amount of money to spend on this new hobby.
First talk about the things he can buy to help him learn the language.
Then say which will be the best use of his money.

Talk to your partner.
Talk about the situation – not about yourself!
Say what you think – explain why.
Ask for your partner's opinions.

Look at these ways of starting the discussion.
Where shall we begin?
Let's talk about x first.
How about ..., what do you think of that idea?

Look at these ways of saying what you think.
I think ... is a good idea because ...
I think ... is better than ... because ...
I think s/he should buy ... because ...
I think the best thing (for him/her) to buy is ... because ...

Look at these ways of responding to what your partner says.
That's a good idea because ...
I'm not so sure about that because ...
And what do you think about ...?

Get ready for PET Speaking Part 2

1 Listen to the instructions. Are you talking about yourself or somebody else?
2 Speak to your partner, not to the examiner.
3 Remember to *listen* to your partner and *respond* to what s/he says.
4 Say *what* you think and explain *why* you think it.

2 **Pietro and Valerie are doing exercise 3.1. Complete the gaps in their conversation using the phrases below. Write the correct letters in the spaces.**

Valerie: So, our friend wants to learn a new language?
Pietro: **(1)** ....
Valerie: No, he can't. Let's start by talking about which of them will be useful for him.
Pietro: **(2)** ....
Valerie: OK. Shall we start with this one, the dictionary?
Pietro: **(3)** ....
Valerie: Yes, I agree, and it's also good for checking spelling. But what about a textbook? They're useful too.
Pietro: **(4)** ....
Valerie: Possibly. Or he may get one free when he pays for the course.
Pietro: **(5)** ....

Use five of these phrases to complete Pietro's part of the conversation.

A Oh yes, that's a good point.
B I don't like them very much.
C Yes they are, but maybe he won't need one because he'll have a teacher.
D Would you like a dictionary or a textbook?
E OK, then afterwards we can decide which one he should buy.
F That's right, and he's only got £20 to spend, so he can't buy all these things, can he?
G Yes, I think he should buy one of those, because it's very useful if you don't know what words mean.

1.5 3 **Which two phrases didn't you use? Now listen and check.**

4 Listening 1.6

- Look at these five sentences.
- Listen to Tim and Janet talking about the courses they are doing in their free time.
- Decide if each sentence is correct or incorrect.
- If you think it is correct, put a tick (✓) in the box under **A** for **Yes**. If you think it is not correct, put a tick (✓) in the box under **B** for **No**.

		A Yes	B No
1	Janet thinks her computer classes are too long.	☐	☐
2	Tim has learnt many new things on his course.	☐	☐
3	Tim has to buy the food he cooks on his course.	☐	☐
4	Tim asks Janet to help him with his cookery.	☐	☐
5	Janet agrees to help Tim solve a problem.	☐	☐

5 Writing

Complete the second sentence so that it means the same as the first, using no more than three words.

1 Each lesson lasts two hours.
Each lesson .... long.
2 What's the price of this CD-ROM, please?
How .... this CD-ROM cost, please?
3 I think a dictionary is very useful.
A dictionary is very useful .... opinion.
4 I think you are right about the textbook.
I agree .... you about the textbook.
5 Let's talk about the videotape first.
How .... about the videotape first?

2 2 All the best books

1 Reading

Read the notices and answer the questions.

- Which one can you probably see in **a)** a library? **b)** a bookshop?
- Which one is **a)** advertising something? **b)** warning you?
- What does each notice mean? Choose **A, B** or **C**.

1

Just published
Mediterranean Cookery
by **Poppy Tobin**
Signed copies available on request

A We have published all of Poppy Tobin's books about cooking.

B Sign here if you'd like a copy of Poppy Tobin's latest book.

C Buy a new book with the writer's signature in it here.

2

Please respect all books in your care.
Heavy fines for any damage to borrowed books.

A Take care when looking at damaged books.

B You'll have to pay if you don't look after our books.

C You can use these books here, but you can't borrow them.

2 Vocabulary

Look at these book covers. What type of book do you think each one is? Choose your answers from the words in the box.

mystery	romance	horror	science fiction
thriller	biography	humour	travel

Which of these books would you like to read? Why do you enjoy this type of book?

3 Reading

The people in 1–5 all want to buy a book.

- Look at the descriptions of eight books (A–H).
- Decide which one would be most suitable for each person.

Underline the words that describe what is important for each person. Only ONE book will match ALL these details.

1 Laura is looking for a book for her grandson's fifth birthday present. Preferably, it should be about space travel or animals and be a story she can read to him many times.

2 Moira's 14-year-old daughter loves science fiction videos. Moira wants to encourage her to read more by giving her a book which will hold her attention.

3 Fiona, like everyone in her family, is very interested in the cinema and enjoys reading about it. She wants a book that will give her all the gossip about film stars past and present.

4 James, who is 15, is looking for something to pass the time on a long plane journey. He'd like to read an adventure story which brings a period of history to life.

5 Gerry likes mystery stories which are full of suspense and excitement. He'd prefer to buy a book by a new writer.

This week's bargain books

A The Meeting
This exciting novel is aimed at teenagers but adults will enjoy it, too. It's the 16th century and Per, the farm boy, rescues a princess. There are marvellous chases, battle scenes and romantic meetings – you couldn't ask for more thrilling action in a story, or a more realistic picture of the past.

B Stealing Scenes
Starting at the age of five, the writer of this amusing autobiography has had a long and successful career as an actress on stage and screen. She takes us into her world of lights and cameras and tells the secrets of famous people she has known.

C The Bucketful of Dinosaurs
When Harry finds a bucketful of dinosaurs, he's delighted and takes them everywhere he goes until one day he leaves them on a train. How will he prove that the dinosaurs belong to him? Very young children will never get tired of listening to this charming adventure.

D Blood Rain
In this seventh book in the series about an Italian police inspector, the hero investigates a murder. The victim? Maybe just a friendless nobody, or perhaps the son of the country's most powerful criminal. Can the inspector manage both to find the murderer and to stay alive?

E Hex Shadows
This story is set in the year 2367 when Britain is a part of the cruel European Federation. Hexes, human computers who were created in the late 21st century, are now hunted down as enemies of the Federation. This is an exciting, fast-moving story which teenagers will love.

F Space Age
Designed with the fact-hungry child in mind, this gives information about stars, galaxies, astronauts and spaceships. It will bring the universe to life and make science and technology fun for those between five and ten years old.

G Stormy Weather
This thriller is the first from the pen of a young Canadian. It follows the story of Dale, a meteorologist who is invited on a small plane to watch a thunderstorm. Dale soon discovers that not all dangers come from nature, and to save his life he must find the answers to some deadly questions.

H Shoot!
For more than 20 years, this has been recognized as the best guide to the movies. This latest edition gives details and opinions about more than 22,000 films. It tells you about video and DVD availability, which films are suitable for family viewing, and the prizes films have won.

Get ready for PET Reading Part 2

1 Look at the information about Laura. Underline the words that are important about her.
Have you underlined: *grandson's fifth birthday, space travel or animals* and *read … many times*?
2 Which book would be suitable for a child of five (*grandson's fifth birthday*)? Are A, B or E suitable? Why not?
What about C and F? Why? (*very young children, those between five and ten years old*)
3 Are C and F about *space travel* or *animals*? Remember, dinosaurs are animals.
4 C and F can't both be suitable. Which one is unsuitable? Why? So which is the most suitable book for Laura?
5 Now do the same for the other people.

4 Vocabulary

Harry had a *bucketful* of dinosaurs. Complete these sentences in an interesting way.

1 Brian can't speak because he's just taken a mouthful of ....
2 You won't get better unless you swallow this spoonful of ....
3 When nobody was looking, Katia gave me a handful of ....
4 Graham felt hungry when he looked at the plateful of ....
5 Jenny's jacket was heavy because she had a pocketful of ....

5 Writing

1 **This is a story called 'The Strange Visitor'. The sentences aren't in the right order. Read the sentences and put them in the correct order. The first one has been done for you.**

☐ She knew what she had to do.
☐ Jenny cried out in surprise and the strange visitor disappeared.
☐ Although the person didn't speak, Jenny could hear some words in her head.
[1] One day when Jenny arrived home, she saw someone standing at her front door, hidden underneath a large, old-fashioned coat and hat.
☐ To prepare for that day, you must study hard and learn all you can.'
☐ She went inside, took out her homework and studied all evening.
☐ She didn't know why, but she felt that this person was very old, wise and kind.
☐ 'This is only my first visit, and when we meet again I will show you my home on a distant planet.

2 **Now you are going to write your own story. It is also called 'The Strange Visitor', but it must be a *different* story.**

Before you start to write, answer these questions about your own story.

- Who does the visitor come to see?
- Where and when does the visit happen?
- What is strange about the visitor?
- How does the person visited feel about the visitor?
- What happens in the end?

3 **Write your story in about 100 words.**

3 1 Holiday adventures

1 Reading

Read these notices. Which one can you see a) in a travel agency window? b) at an airport? c) in a hotel?

1

Find out about excursions, nightlife and transport to the airport at our 24-hour reception desk

2

70,000 package holidays
Reservations 9 am – 6 pm

Leave an answerphone message outside these hours

3

Do not leave your luggage unattended at any time

What does each notice mean? Choose A, B or C.

A Make sure there's always someone with your belongings.

B You can make a booking here during the day.

C Someone is always available to give you information.

2 Speaking

1 **Look at picture A and answer these questions. Use the words in the box.**

1 Who can you see in the picture?
2 Where is she?
3 What's she doing?
4 What things can you see in the picture?
5 How does the girl probably feel? Why?

suitcase	young	wearing	packing
bedroom	nervous	clothes	holiday
quilt	abroad	plastic	woman

A

2 **Now use your answers to describe the picture.**
Begin: *This picture shows a young woman in her bedroom. She's ...*

3 **Now look at picture B. Describe what you can see in the picture. Talk about:**

- where the picture was taken
- the people
- what they are doing
- the things you can see
- what they are probably talking about

Use these words:

jacket	phone	writing
curly	arrangements	brochures
discussing	travel agency	shelf
desk	trip	pen

B

Begin: *This picture shows two people in a travel agency. They're ...*

3 Reading

Don't worry if you don't understand some words.

Do the sentences match what the text says?

1 **Would you like to go on an adventure holiday? Read about a scuba-diving boat tour to see if it could be the holiday for you.**

2 **Read the text to decide if each sentence is correct or incorrect.**

1 The giant tortoises in the Galapagos Islands are over 120 years old.
2 The Galapagos penguins live further north than any other penguins.
3 You can always be sure of seeing whales in the Galapagos.
4 There's so much to see in the Galapagos that you should stay at least seven days.
5 Divers get the chance to go walking on Darwin Island.
6 It's safe to go looking for sharks round Wolf Rocks if you're new to diving.
7 On the boats, passengers have sleeping accommodation on two different levels.
8 Each boat has a total of five members of staff.
9 If you like, you can go to the Andes after you've finished diving in the Galapagos.
10 You can use the Internet to book a holiday in the Galapagos.

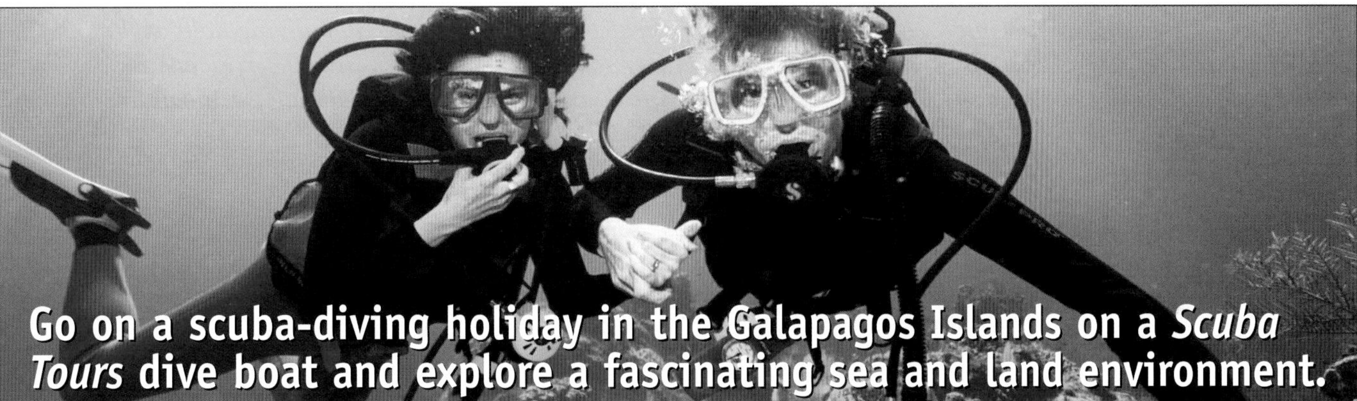

Go on a scuba-diving holiday in the Galapagos Islands on a *Scuba Tours* dive boat and explore a fascinating sea and land environment.

The Galapagos Islands

These extraordinary islands lie in the Pacific Ocean, 1,000 kilometres off the coast of Ecuador. Some of the world's strangest creatures live here, for example giant tortoises that can reach 120 years in age and marine iguanas that look like prehistoric dinosaurs. The Galapagos are also home to penguins (nowhere else are they found so far north) and sea ea lions. Underwater it is a paradise for divers and snorkellers. A flow of cold water from the south meets a flow of warm water from the north, meaning it is possible to find a huge range of sea life. Hammerhead sharks suddenly appear out of nowhere, and, at certain times of year, whales pass by the islands. The wildlife and scenery is so varied here that a seven-day voyage is the minimum you should consider, and we recommend 14 days to get the most from the experience.

Diving opportunities

Our tour starts at San Cristobal and we travel northwards, past North Seymour Island to Wolf and Darwin Islands. This route offers some of the most spectacular diving opportunities in the world. There are three or four dives every day and one or two land tours, except at Wolf and Darwin as landing there is forbidden. Divers usually mention visits to Mosquera (for the sea lions) and Bartolome (for the penguins) as highlights. Wolf Rocks is a favourite place to see sharks, though this site is not suitable for inexperienced divers.

The accommodation

Scuba Tours has two boats, Sea Bird and Sea Wind. Each boat is 30 metres in length and has four levels. On the lowest level, there are four cabins to accommodate eight people. Above this is the main deck where there is a comfortable sitting and dining area. On the upper deck, there are three more double cabins, and above this an open-air sun deck. A crew of five look after you on board, and a further four crew members take care of you when you are in the water or on land tours.

Additional land tours

On request, we can arrange a variety of additional land tours on the mainland of Ecuador. These tours include four days in the Amazon rainforest, a visit to volcanoes in the Andes mountains, and trips to some fascinating markets. Apart from the Amazon tour, which has fixed departure dates, these can be added at the start or end of any Galapagos diving holiday.

Prices and booking

For current prices and an online reservation form, visit our website at www.scubatours.com.

Get ready for PET Reading Part 3

1 Don't worry about the meaning of every word. You don't have to understand every word in the text, only the ones which help you do the task.
2 Use the headings to help you find the answers. In which paragraphs can you find the answers to sentences 6, 7, 9 and 10?
3 Underline the words in the text which help you with each sentence. Which words will you underline for sentences 1, 2, 3 and 4?
4 Decide if the words in the text and the sentence have the same meaning. Look at number 1. Does *The giant tortoises ... are over 120 years old* mean the same as *giant tortoises ... can reach 120 years in age*? What about number 2? Does it mean the same as *The Galapagos are also home to penguins (nowhere else are they found so far north)*?

4 Writing

There are several ways to say *when* something happens.
Examples:
You must get a scuba-diving certificate ***before*** *you can go on a diving holiday.*
You can go on a diving holiday ***after*** *you have got a scuba-diving certificate.*
You can't go on a diving holiday ***until*** *you have got a scuba-diving certificate.*

When *the divers reached Wolf Rocks they saw some sharks.*
The divers saw some sharks ***as soon as*** *they reached Wolf Rocks.*

People make a lot of new friends ***while*** *they're on a scuba-diving holiday.*
People make a lot of new friends ***during*** *a scuba-diving holiday.*

Complete the second sentence so that it means the same as the first, using no more than three words.

1 Learn to ski before you go on a winter holiday in the mountains.
Don't go on a winter holiday in the mountains until .... to ski.
2 When we arrived at the hotel, we immediately went for a swim.
We went for a swim as .... we arrived at the hotel.
3 We'll go sightseeing after lunch.
We'll go sightseeing when .... had lunch.
4 During my holiday in Paris, I spoke a lot of French.
I spoke a lot of French while I .... in Paris.
5 Don't book your holiday until you've seen my photos of Africa.
You must see my photos of Africa .... your holiday.

5 Vocabulary

You can use the words in the box when you're talking about holidays. Divide them into the six groups.

~~hotel~~ countryside ~~sunglasses~~ shells plane taking photos ~~swimming~~ coach ~~postcards~~ train guest house ~~car~~ sunbathing tent suntan lotion handicrafts ~~beach~~ guidebook picnics

Transport	Accommodation	Scenery	Activities	Things to pack	Souvenirs
car	*hotel*	*beach*	*swimming*	*sunglasses*	*postcards*

Think of words which describe the kind of holiday you like most. Use a dictionary to help you. Add the words to the table.

6 Speaking

Talk about the kind of holidays you like and don't like.

3.2 Just the job

1 Reading

Read these messages. What does each one say? Choose A, B or C.

1

```
E-mail:
To:    Ronan
From:  David
Several members of staff are
wearing jeans with their
uniform jackets, which they
know is against company
rules. Can you speak to
them? Thanks.
```

The boss wants Ronan to

A inform staff about new company rules.

B ask staff for their opinion of the company uniform.

C warn staff their appearance isn't satisfactory.

2

Ronan,

During the bus strike next week, I can give you a lift to the office. Shall I pick you up at 7 o'clock?

Maddy

What is Maddy offering to do for Ronan?

A drive him to work

B wake him up early

C accompany him on the bus

Do you think Ronan will be happy to receive these messages? What kinds of things make people happy or unhappy at work?

2 Vocabulary

1 **Many people have to study for several years before they take up a profession or job. For example, an *architect* has studied *architecture*, and a *doctor* has studied *medicine*. What have these people studied?**

Profession	Subject studied
architect	*architecture*
doctor	*medicine*
lawyer	
artist	
cook	
engineer	
tourist guide	
hairdresser	
journalist	
businesswoman	
actor	
chemist	
biologist	
physicist	
musician	

2 **Look at these verbs. You can make nouns by changing the end of each one. Complete the table.**

Verb	Noun
apply	*application*
organize	
qualify	
decide	
operate	
employ	*employment*
advertise	
govern	
manage	
retire	
insure	
succeed	

Use the pairs of words to make sentences.
Example:
If you want to apply for a job, you have to fill in an application form.

3 Listening

1.7–10 **1** **You will hear four women talking about their jobs. Listen and complete the information in the table.**

Speaker	Clothes	Equipment	Place	Activity
1				*controlling traffic*
2			*advertising agency*	
3		*microscope*		
4				

Listen again and match the speakers with the pictures, A, B, C or D.

A

B

C

D

3 Listening

1.11 **2 You will hear a woman talking on the radio about her job. Put a tick (✓) in the correct box for each question.**

Read all the questions quickly first.

1 Where does Amanda usually work?
A ☐ in a restaurant
B ☐ in her own kitchen
C ☐ in recording studios

Be ready to listen for the answer to the next question even if you have missed the answer to the first one.

2 People are satisfied with Amanda's service because
A ☐ she provides large meals.
B ☐ she cooks healthy food.
C ☐ she prepares unusual dishes.

3 Amanda finds her job stressful if she
A ☐ has to work in unsuitable places.
B ☐ doesn't know when she should serve a meal.
C ☐ doesn't know how many people to cook for.

4 What does Amanda enjoy most about her job?
A ☐ meeting famous bands
B ☐ working for young people
C ☐ earning a lot of money

5 How does Amanda get to the place where she works?
A ☐ by car **B** ☐ by bus **C** ☐ on foot

You can answer any questions you've missed when you hear the recording for a second time.

6 When she gets home in the evening, Amanda
A ☐ writes about cooking.
B ☐ cooks for her family.
C ☐ listens to music.

Get ready for PET Listening Part 2

1 Listen to the instructions.
- How many people will you hear?
- Who are they?
- What are they talking about?

2 Read the questions quickly before you listen.
The questions are in the same order as the recording.
- Underline the most important word(s) in the question.
- Don't read the A, B, C options yet.

3 Listen to the recording. Can you hear the answers to the questions?
- Tick the box which best answers the question.

4 Listen again. Check that your answers are correct.

Remember:
- the questions are in the same order as the information on the recording.
- the answer will not always use exactly the same words as the recording.
- you may hear the words in all the options A, B, C on the recording.
- only one option, A, B or C answers the question.

4 Writing

Write a story which begins with this sentence:

Denis wanted to earn some money during the school holidays so he asked his uncle for a job.

Before you start to write, answer these questions.
- Where did Denis get a job?
- What kind of work did he do there?
- Who did he work with?
- How did he feel about the job?
- What happened unexpectedly one day?
- What did Denis do?

Write your story in about 100 words.

4.1 House and home

1 Vocabulary

1 **Which rooms do you have in your house?**

dining room	kitchen	bedroom	garage
living room	bathroom	hallway	balcony
garden	stairs	storeroom	basement

Do you have any other rooms in your house?

2 **In which room do you usually find these things? Divide them into the four groups. Some words can be used more than once.**

dishwasher	wardrobe	chest of drawers	sink
coffee table	washbasin	armchair	dressing table
television	lamp	fridge	shower
cooker	towel rail	mirror	sofa

Living room	Kitchen	Bathroom	Bedroom

2 Speaking

1 **In the Speaking test, you talk about a photograph. If you don't know the word for something, you can say what it looks like, or what it is used for.**

Example:

What's a coffee table?

It's a small, low table which you usually find in the living room. You can put things like cups of coffee, newspapers and magazines on it.

Talk about these things in the same way:

- a chest of drawers
- a towel rail
- a dishwasher
- a wardrobe
- a vase

2 **Choose one of the photographs opposite and describe the room. Use the words in the box to help you talk about:**

- the type of room it is
- what you can see in the room
- where the things are
- your opinion of the room
- who you think lives there

there's a/some
on top of
next to/beside
underneath/below
to the right of
to the left of
behind
in front of

A

B

3 Listening 1.12

1 **Listen to a boy describing his room. Which room is his?**

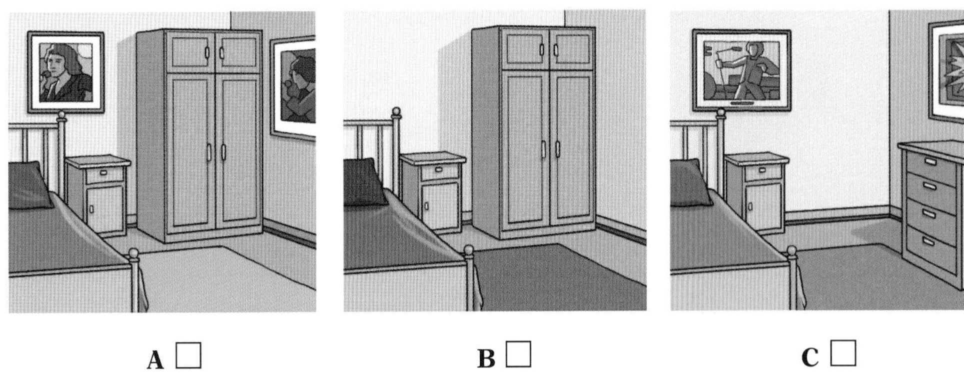

A ☐ B ☐ C ☐

2 **Describe your house. Talk about:**

- where it is
- what it looks like
- how many rooms it has
- your favourite room

4 Writing

Your English penfriend, who's called Chris, has never visited you and has asked you what your room is like.
Write a letter to Chris. In your letter, you should

- tell him how big your room is
- say what is in the room
- explain why you like it

Write 35–45 words.

5 Listening 1.13–16

You hear each recording twice.

Read the questions carefully.

Only one picture answers the question.

1 **Look at the three pictures. Where is the mobile phone in each picture?**

A ☐ **B** ☐ **C** ☐

2 **What time does the film start?**

A ☐ **B** ☐ **C** ☐

3 **What does the woman decide to eat?**

A ☐ **B** ☐ **C** ☐

4 **Which piece of equipment does the woman need?**

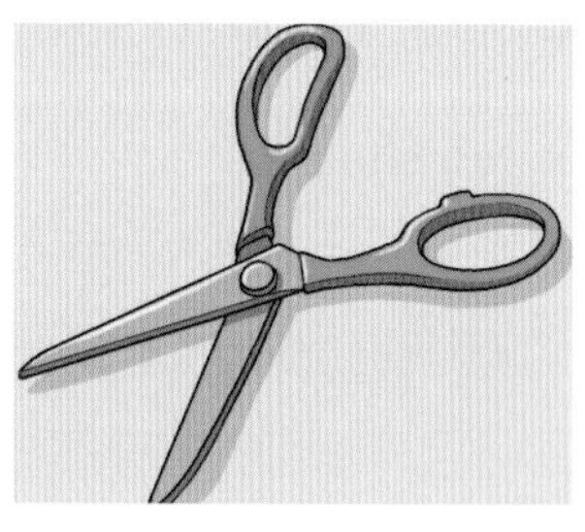
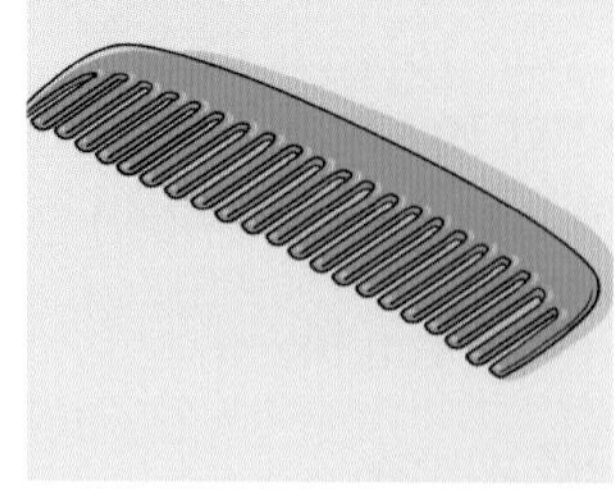

A ☐ **B** ☐ **C** ☐

4.2 Interesting people

1 Vocabulary

1 **How often does your family get together for a celebration? Do you enjoy family parties? Why? Why not?**

2 **Find someone in the photo who:**

is fair-haired	has curly hair	is in blue jeans	is smiling
is middle-aged	looks tired	is wearing glasses	is pointing

Now describe the photo. Begin like this:

'This is a picture of a family party. There are people of all ages here. Most of them are sitting down at a table, but two men …'

3 **The words in the boxes describe people. In the first box, find seven pairs of words with *opposite* meanings.**

attractive	careful	careless	cheerful	confident	miserable	foolish
hard-working	lazy	shy	strong	ugly	weak	wise

4 **In this box, find seven pairs of words with *similar* meanings.**

amusing	anxious	blond	boring	understanding	dull	fair
funny	honest	patient	slim	thin	truthful	worried

5 **Which words describe you?**

2 Writing

You had arranged to meet your cousin at the station, but now you can't go. Write an e-mail to Robin, your English friend. In your e-mail, you should

- ask Robin to meet your cousin for you
- say why you can't go
- describe your cousin

Write 35–45 words.

3 Reading

1 Generally, how old are people when they first a) learn to read? b) go to university? Read the article about a boy who has done these things at a younger age than most people, and then answer the questions.

The most difficult thing for university student Shaun Rogers is opening his classroom door. Shaun can't do this without help because he's only six years old. He's the youngest person ever to study at Rochester University in New York. Shaun began reading at two, and by four was knowledgeable about a range of subjects from astronomy to zoology. By the age of five, he was regularly corresponding with university professors about his ideas. He has just completed his first book which will be published in a few months, shortly after his seventh birthday. 'I love learning,' says Shaun. 'My hero is the scientist Albert Einstein because he never combed his hair or wore socks.'

Psychologists have found it difficult to test Shaun's intelligence because it goes beyond what they usually measure. Shaun's mother first realized her son was different when he kept crying at playschool because he was bored with the children's games. She started teaching him at home after finding that local schools were not prepared for children who learnt at Shaun's speed. Now Shaun is studying geography at Rochester University and using the Internet to complete his high school studies.

However, some psychologists warn that too much study can prevent a child from developing normally. 'I don't care how brilliant the kid is, six-year-olds have to play with their friends,' says Dr Brian Wood. Mrs Rogers disagrees that her son's time is completely taken up by school work. 'He loves the violin and has many outdoor interests, such as camping, fishing and swimming, just like other boys his age.'

This question is asking you about the writer's purpose.

1 What is the writer trying to do in the text?
A advise parents about their children's education
B compare the development of normal and clever children
C encourage students to enter university at a young age
D interest people in the life of an unusual child

2 How old was Shaun when he wrote his first book?
A four
B five
C six
D seven

3 Why did Shaun's mother decide to educate him at home?
A because she couldn't find a suitable school for him
B because his school wouldn't let him use the Internet
C because his teachers were unkind and made him cry
D because he didn't get on with the other children

This question is asking you about Dr Wood's opinion.

4 What does Dr Wood think about Shaun?
A He isn't really any cleverer than other six-year-olds.
B He should spend more time having fun with other children.
C He will have to study harder to succeed at university.
D He can help his friends to do better at school.

You need to look at the whole text to answer this question.

5 Which of these is Mrs Rogers talking about Shaun?
A 'My son gets bored easily if he doesn't have other children to play games or go swimming with him.'
B 'My son loves his studies and fortunately there are many children of his own age in his class who share his interests.'
C 'What makes my son different from other children is that he started studying earlier and learns things much more quickly.'
D 'Like most young boys, my son often looks untidy and spends more time using the Internet than doing his homework.'

Get ready for PET Reading Part 4

1 The first question on this kind of reading text asks you about the writer's purpose. Has the writer of the text about Shaun succeeded in her/his purpose? In other words, has s/he interested you in Shaun's life?
2 In this kind of reading text, you have to understand people's *attitudes* and *opinions* as well as factual information. From this text, what do you understand about:
- Shaun's *attitude* to studying?
- Dr Wood's *opinion* about what six-year-old children need to do?
- Mrs Rogers' *opinion* about the amount of time her son spends studying?

3 In some of the questions in this kind of reading text, you have to look for the answer in more than one place. Look at question 5 and underline the two places in the text which give you the correct answer.

2 **Match the writer's purposes with the sentences.**

1 to recommend something
2 to compare two things
3 to complain about something
4 to explain something
5 to warn against something

A Couples who decide to adopt a child should be prepared for the time when the child starts to ask difficult questions about the birth parents.
B Why do people using mobile phones in public places imagine everyone is interested in their conversations and speak in very loud voices?
C If, like me, you enjoy a film which keeps you sitting on the edge of your seat, then you shouldn't miss this one.
D I felt close to my grandmother because she always met me from school and listened while I described the events of my day.
E Children with several brothers and sisters may feel differently from an only child when it comes to the school holidays.

4 Writing

Complete the second sentence so that it means the same as the first, using no more than three words.
1 That teacher is very patient with her students.
That is the teacher .... very patient with her students.
2 Shaun is too weak to open the classroom door.
Shaun isn't .... to open the classroom door.
3 In our class, only a few students have curly hair.
In our class, not .... curly hair.
4 My brother prefers funny films to serious ones.
My brother likes funny films .... serious ones.
5 'My favourite film star is Tom Cruise,' said my grandmother.
'Tom Cruise is the film star I like ....,' said my grandmother.

5 1 Places of interest

1 Reading

1 Look at the notices, 1–10. Would you find them in a museum, a sports centre, a hotel, a giftshop or a post office?

1 **Last collection:** 19.30 Mon–Fri.

2 *Changing rooms this way*

3 Rooms should be vacated by 12.00

4

5 Parcels and heavy items should be taken to window 7 for weighing

6 *Please do not touch the exhibits*

7 EQUIPMENT CAN BE HIRED BY THE HOUR

8 All breakages must be paid for

9 *Photocopying facilities are available to guests at Reception*

10 *A map of the display areas is available at the entrance*

2 Look at each notice again. Is it:

a) giving you information about what facilities are available?
b) telling you what you must or mustn't do?
c) giving you simple information, for example where or when?

3 Choose one place from the box below. What type of notices would you expect to see there? Write two examples of each type, a), b) and c).

school	department store	bank	airport

2 Listening 1.17–18

Get ready for PET Listening Part 3

1 Listen to the instructions.
- What are you going to listen to?

2 Read the notes quickly before you listen. The questions are in the same order as the recording.
- What type of information are you listening for in each question?
- Can you guess what the answers could be?

3 Listen to the recording. Can you hear the missing information?
- Write the missing information in the space.
- Write only one or two words.

4 Listen again. Check that your answers are correct.

Get ready for PET Listening Part 3

Remember:
- the questions are in the same order as the information on the recording.
- you will hear the word(s) you have to write on the recording.
- you may hear other words that can fit the space – listen carefully.
- don't write more than one or two words (or sometimes a number).
- if the answer is a number, write the figure (for example 5), not the words.

Write only one or two words.
You hear the talk twice.

1 **Look at the notes about Woburn Safari Park.**

- You will hear a talk about a Safari Park.
- For each question, fill in the missing information in the numbered space.

WOBURN SAFARI PARK

It takes **(1)** .... to drive from London to Woburn Safari Park.

You travel around the park in **(2)** ....

In the park, you can see:
- lions and tigers
- giraffes
- elephants
- four different types of **(3)** ....

In the park, you are not allowed to have **(4)** ....

The park is open from Easter until the end of **(5)** .... each year.

After your tour of the park, you can visit:
- the children's playground
- the education centre
- the **(6)** ....

2 **Look at the notes about Oxford Castle.**

- You will hear part of a radio programme about the castle.
- For each question, fill in the missing information in the numbered space.

OXFORD CASTLE

How long it has been there:	**(1)** .... *years*
What it was used for in the past:	*it was a* **(2)** ....
What most of it is used for now:	*it is a* **(3)** ....
The main attractions for visitors:	*museum and* **(4)** ....
What you can do on the summer evenings:	**(5)** .... *in the open air*
Number to call for more information:	**(6)** ....

3 Reading

Look at the sentences about the Florida Keys area of the USA. Read the text and decide if each sentence is correct or incorrect.

1 The Florida Keys have a lot in common with other tourist attractions in Florida.
2 The main road through the islands is 200 miles long.
3 There are good opportunities to do underwater sports around the islands.
4 Visitors can choose from a wide range of places to stay in the islands.
5 The writer says that a good way to see the islands is to drive there from Miami.
6 Key West is a good place if you're looking for a relaxing life.
7 Mallory Dock is popular with local people as well as tourists.
8 It's a good idea to eat fish when you visit Mallory Dock.
9 You can see most of the Florida Keys in a short holiday.

THE FLORIDA KEYS

When you think of Florida, what comes to mind? Probably images of Disneyland, package holidays and burgers with extra relish. Well, the islands known as the Florida Keys couldn't be more unlike the mainland and that's one of the best kept secrets in the USA. Located between the Atlantic and the Gulf of Mexico, the Florida Keys are a line of islands that runs for 200 miles from the tip of Florida out into the ocean. The last island is just 90 miles away from the coast of Cuba. Along the way, there are islands, reefs, lakes, bays and beaches. From the largest island, Key Largo, to the tip of Key West, there are 43 bridges on the 126-mile Overseas Highway.

There really is something for everybody in the Florida Keys: excellent diving, a good range of theatres, museums, shops and restaurants; and every type of accommodation, from country camping places and family-owned guesthouses to the most luxurious hotels.

A good way to see the Keys is to take a flight from Miami to Key West, which takes half an hour. You can then hire a car and drive back to Miami, stopping at all the main attractions along the way. As you travel, you'll notice the green-and-white mile markers telling you how far you've come and how far you have to go.

Key West, the southernmost part of the USA, has a very laid-back attitude. For over a hundred years, it has been home to all sorts of people who want to avoid the stress of the mainland, especially artists and writers.

One part of the city you'll want to see is Mallory Dock, where the performances of street entertainers are enjoyed by locals and tourists alike. Once the sun has gone down, the open-air restaurants and bars come alive. Local seafood is superb and varied. If you're really brave you can even try fried alligator tail or, if you prefer, you can just dance all night.

To make the most of the food and culture on all the islands, you'd need to make your stay a long one. In fact, one of the most surprising things about Florida Keys is the number of visitors who decide to stay far longer than they had originally planned – some like it so much that they never go home again!

4 Speaking

1 **What are the main tourist attractions in your area**

- for young people?
- for older people?
- for foreign visitors?

2 **Talk about a historic building in your country and say what visitors can see and do there.**

5 2

Getting there

1 Vocabulary

1 Look at the words in the box. Divide them into four groups. Some of the words can be used more than once.

driver	pilot	attendant	land	catch	miss
get on	take off	check in	ticket	fare	station
take	platform	boarding pass	meter	timetable	gate

Taxi	Train	Bus/Coach	Plane

2 Complete the gaps in these sentences with words from the table.

1 If we don't hurry up, we'll .... the bus. It leaves the bus .... at ten o'clock.
2 It's cheaper for four people to .... a taxi rather than go on the underground, because the taxi .... comes to less than the price of four ....
3 After you .... your luggage, they give you a .... which you take along to the ...., where someone checks it before you .... the plane.
4 The train to Edinburgh leaves from .... number eight and you have to buy your .... in the office before you ....
5 In the ...., it said that the bus left at 10.00, and so we got there at 09.45 so that we would be sure to .... it.

2 Speaking

Look at the photograph and describe it. Make sure you answer these questions:

- Where was it taken? Who are the people? What is each of them doing? Why?
- What things can you see in the photograph?
- What are the people going to do next? Why?

What are the good and bad things about travelling by plane?

3 Reading

1 Look at these notices. On which type of transport would you expect to see each one?

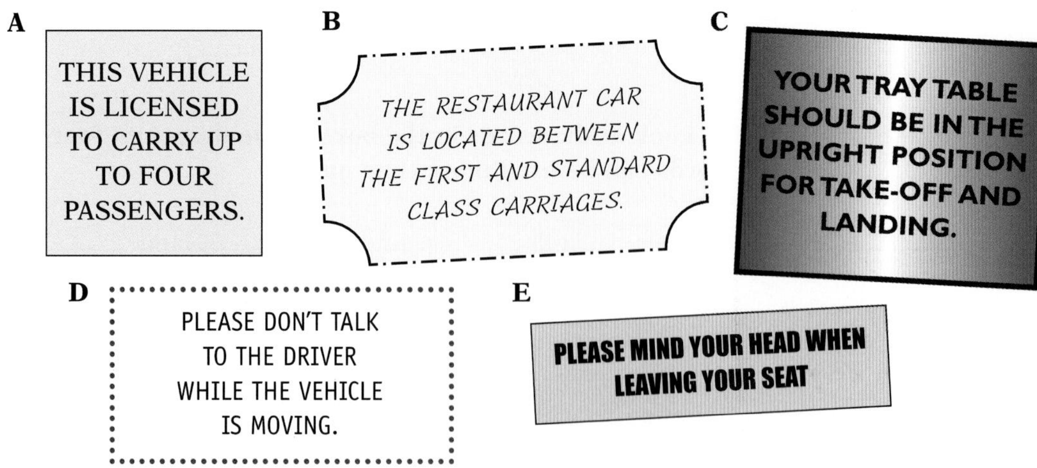

Get ready for PET Reading Part 1

1 In Part 1 of the PET Reading test, there are five multiple-choice (**A**, **B** or **C**) questions.

2 You have to look at either a public notice or a personal message and answer the question about it. The message may be an e-mail or a handwritten note. The notice may be:

- telling you what to do or not to do
- telling you what is available
- giving you information about things

3 This is how to choose the correct explanation:

- First look at the notice or message and imagine how you would explain it to a friend.
- Then look at the three explanations and choose which one is closest to what you would say.
- Finally, check the other explanations and find words and phrases in the notice that tell you that these explanations are incorrect.

2 Look at this notice. Choose the correct explanation, A, B or C.

Available 1st July.
One-bedroom furnished flat.
Reasonable rent.
Convenient for shops and buses.

A I'm looking for somewhere to live.
B I'm looking for furniture for a flat.
C I'm looking for someone to live in a flat.

The answer to this question is C.
Which words tell you that this is the answer?
Which words tell you that **A** is not the answer?
Which words tell you that **B** is not the answer?

3 Look at these notices and messages and decide which is the correct explanation, A, B or C. Think about why your answers are correct and why the others are incorrect.

1 *PLEASE SPEAK QUIETLY IN THE LIBRARY AREA. PEOPLE ARE STUDYING NEARBY.*

A You are not allowed to talk here.
B You can only stay here if you are studying.
C You should try not to disturb people.

2

Hot and cold snacks served all day.

A Sit down and a waiter will come to serve you.

B You can buy drinks here, but not food.

C You can get a light meal here.

3

E-mail:

To: Yolanda
From: Tina

Did I leave a book in your car? The thing is, it's not mine – I borrowed it from my brother who now wants it back!

What does Tina want Yolanda to do?

A return the book she borrowed

B lend her a book

C look for a book she has lost

4

Telephone message

To: Luca

From: Matteo

The football match is going to be on Saturday this week, instead of Sunday. Usual time and place. Everyone else can still play. OK for you?

This week's football match

A will take place on a different day.

B will have some different players.

C will be starting later than usual.

5

ALL VISITORS SHOULD REPORT TO THE OFFICE ON ARRIVAL.

A Please go to the office before you leave.

B Please call the office to make an appointment.

C Please go to the office when you first come here.

4 Writing

You are going to visit an English friend called Jo, who lives in a big city. Send an e-mail to Jo. In your e-mail, you should

- say how you will travel
- tell her what time you will arrive
- say what you'd like to do during your visit

Write 35–45 words.

6 1 What a bargain!

1 Vocabulary

What's the difference between these pairs of words?
Example:
A jacket is shorter than a coat.
Check your answers in a dictionary.

coat/jacket	shirt/skirt
boot/shoe	socks/tights
tie/belt	wool/cotton
collar/sleeve	spots/stripes
pocket/bag	zip/buttons

2 Reading

Read these notices. Match them with the correct explanation, A, B, C or D. There is one extra explanation.

1

Changing rooms next to lift. Customers may take in no more than 4 pieces of clothing.

2

Sorry! Lift to women's fashions out of order – Use escalator in TV department

3

Today only! Prices on all electrical goods greatly reduced

A Because the lift isn't working, you'll have to go upstairs another way.

B You may not change any women's clothes you buy in today's sale.

C If you buy a television today, it will be much cheaper than usual.

D There's a limit to the number of clothes you may try on at one time.

3 Vocabulary

Read the sentences about money and find the missing words in the word square. They are written from top to bottom, left to right, right to left and diagonally.

1 I don't _ _ _ _ a lot of money in my job, but I _ _ _ _ some every week for my holiday.
2 If you don't have cash, you can write a _ _ _ _ _ _ or pay by _ _ _ _ _ _ card.
3 If you don't put that _ _ _ _ in your wallet, and the _ _ _ _ in your pocket, you'll lose them before you can spend them!
4 I got a _ _ _ _ _ _ _ when I bought these books for you, so you can see how much money you _ _ _ me.
5 Some people will borrow money from you, but they'll never _ _ _ _ it to you!
6 People like to _ _ _ _ in big department stores because everything they want is under one roof.
7 How much do you _ _ _ _ _ _ to repair shoes?
8 The service was very good here, so I'm going to leave the waitress a large _ _ _ .

C	S	L	S	A	V	E
H	C	H	E	Q	U	E
A	O	R	O	N	X	A
R	I	W	E	P	D	R
G	N	X	E	D	I	N
E	T	O	N	P	I	T
R	E	C	E	I	P	T

4 Writing

1 **In PET Writing Part 3, you may write a letter to an English-speaking friend. Look at this example writing task.**

This is part of a letter you receive from an English penfriend.

I wanted to buy a T-shirt this morning but I had to go food shopping instead, which I hate. Do you like shopping? Are there any good stores near you?

Now write a letter answering your penfriend's questions.
Write your letter in about 100 words.

2 **This is the letter one student wrote. Write the missing words.**

Dear Chris,
Thank you **(1)** .... your letter. I agree **(2)** .... you about food shopping. I hate **(3)** ...., too. The supermarket **(4)** .... always crowded and it's boring looking for rice **(5)** .... coffee!
But I love shopping **(6)** .... clothes even though I **(7)** .... not got much money. My friends and I often **(8)** .... to the shopping centre in my town just to try **(9)** .... clothes. The shop assistants aren't very pleased when **(10)** .... don't buy anything!
I also enjoy **(11)** .... to a music store in the shopping centre. I **(12)** .... hours there listening to **(13)** .... latest CDs. I always buy something, even if it's only **(14)** .... music magazine.
Please write to **(15)** .... again soon.
Love,
Angela

- What is the topic of this letter? Is it what the 'English penfriend' wanted to hear about?
- What different kinds of shopping does Angela mention?
- What *reasons* does Angela give for disliking food shopping?
- What *examples* does Angela give of things she does when she's shopping?
- You start a letter with *'Dear …'* followed by a 'hello' sentence. What 'hello' sentence does Angela use?
- You end a letter with a 'goodbye' sentence. What 'goodbye' sentence does Angela use?
- Look at these sentences. Find three 'hello' sentences and four 'goodbye' sentences.
  'Phone me or e-mail me and tell me what you think.'
  'I'm sorry I haven't written for a long time.'
  'I'm looking forward to your next letter.'
  'I was really pleased to hear your news.'
  'Give my best wishes to your family.'
  'It was great to hear from you again.'
  'See you soon.'
- At the end of a letter, you always sign your name. What does Angela write before her signature? Look at these phrases. Find two from an informal letter and one from a formal one.
  Yours sincerely,
  Best wishes,
  Yours,

Get ready for PET Writing Part 3

1 You have a choice in this part of the test. You have to write either a **letter** or a **story**. Read the instructions for both carefully and decide which one you can write best.
2 If you choose to write the **letter**, you will have to reply to something in a letter from an English penfriend. The penfriend's letter will tell you what the topic of your letter should be. Make sure you know what this topic is, eg 'shopping' or 'clothes'. Also make sure that you write about the topic given, and not about something else. Answer any questions your 'penfriend' asks.
3 In your **letter**, start with '*Dear ...*,' and a 'hello' sentence. You should end with a 'goodbye' sentence, and sign your name.
4 If you choose to write the **story**, you will have either the title or the first sentence to guide you. Ask yourself some questions about your story before you start to write, for example: *Who ... ? Where ... ? When ... ? Why ... ? How did ... feel? What happened in the end?*
5 Your **letter** or **story** will look better if you write it in separate paragraphs, as Angela has done. Start each paragraph on a new line.
6 Try not to write fewer than 100 words, but don't write many more than 100.
7 When you've written your **letter** or **story**, check it carefully. Correct any grammar or spelling mistakes.

Remember to organize your ideas in paragraphs. And check what you have written carefully.

3 **Write this letter.**
This is part of a letter you receive from an English penfriend.

I wore new shoes to a party last night and now my feet hurt. I hate wearing uncomfortable clothes! Tell me about the clothes you like and don't like wearing. What do you wear to parties?

Now write a letter telling your penfriend about the clothes you like.
Write your letter in about 100 words.

5 Listening

1.19 **Do you like shopping in street markets? Why? Why not?**

- Look at the advertisement for some street markets in London.
- Some information is missing.
- Listen to the man talking on the radio about the markets, and fill in the the missing words.

East London Markets

Columbia Road
Over 50 stalls selling (1) .... at bargain prices.

Brick Lane
A market speciality is (2) ....

Petticoat Lane
Sells everything from clothes to toys.
Busiest day is (3) ....

Whitechapel
It's opposite (4) ....
Get your Asian vegetables and spices here.

Come and be part of the fun!

City life

1 Vocabulary

1 **Look at these photographs. Choose one of the photographs and make a list of all the things you can see. Use the ideas to help you.**

A

B

people · colours · objects · clothes · parts of the vehicle · buildings

2 **Answer these questions about your photograph.**

1 What type of vehicle is it?
2 What type of street is it?
3 What are the people in the photo doing?
4 Why are they doing it?
5 How do you think they feel about it?

3 **Now look at the other photograph and answer these questions.**

1 What's the same or similar?
2 What's different?

2 Speaking

1 **Which is better, living in a city or living in the country? Why?**

2 **Look at the adjectives in the box. Which would you use to describe a) living in the city? b) living in the country?**

calm	crowded	peaceful	clean	noisy
dirty	boring	relaxing	stressful	convenient
expensive	exciting	safe	lonely	interesting
fun	dangerous	polluted	inconvenient	

3 **Make lists of the advantages of living in a) the city and b) the country. Use the words in the box to help you.**

shopping	night-life	fresh air	way of life	education
employment	transport	health	entertainment	

4 Talk to another student. Decide who is Student A and who is Student B. Use your lists to have a discussion about life in the two places. Use some of the expressions below.

Student A Try to convince your partner that the city is the best place to live.	**Student B** Try to convince your partner that the country is the best place to live.

One big (dis)advantage of the city/country is that ...

But we have to remember that it is easier to ... in the city/country.

Don't forget that the city/country is much more ... than the country/city.

Another thing is that the city/country is better for ...

I'm afraid I don't agree with you because ...

Yes, you're right, but I still think ...

Get ready for PET Speaking Part 3

1 The examiner gives you a photograph of an everyday situation.
2 You talk on your own for about one minute.
- Tell the examiner everything you can see in the photograph.
- Talk to the examiner, not to your partner.

3 Remember:
- start immediately, and keep talking – don't stop and think.
- talk to the examiner, not your partner.
- talk about everything you can see.
- if you don't know the word for an object in the photograph, say what it looks like, or what it is used for.
- don't stop if you can't think of the word you need; talk about something else in the photograph.

5 When you talk about the photograph, use these ideas to help you.

1 Talk about the *place* in the photograph.
- Is it indoors or outdoors?
- Is it in a house or another building?
- What type of place is it?

2 Talk about the *people* in the photograph.
- How many people are there?
- What do they look like?
- What are they wearing?
- How do they feel?

3 Talk about *what's happening* in the photograph.
- What are the people doing?
- Why are they doing it?

6 **Look at the photograph of some people in the countryside. Talk about it using the ideas in 5.**

Talk to the examiner.

Tell the examiner everything you can see.

7 **Look at the photograph of people in a city and talk about it. Remember:**

- don't talk for more than one minute
- talk about everything you can see in the picture
- don't worry about words you don't know

Your partner will have a different photo.

8 **Talk about a city you know. Say what you like about it and what you don't like about it.**

7 1 Food and drink

1 Vocabulary

1 **Look at the foods in the box. Divide them into the four groups.**

carrots	beans	lamb	peas	onions	garlic
mushrooms	bananas	sausages	grapes	tomatoes	oranges
duck	pasta	beef	rice	chicken	leeks
olives	mayonnaise	tuna	butter	cheese	spinach
pepper	salt	steak	pizza	plums	burgers

Meat and fish	Vegetables	Fruit	Other

2 **Add your favourite foods to the lists.**

2 Speaking

1 **Choose one of the photographs of people eating and talk about it. Remember to talk about everything you can see, including:**

- each person – what they are doing, wearing and feeling
- the food and drink
- other things in the foreground
- things in the background

A

B

2 **What is your favourite food? Talk about:**

- breakfast
- dinner
- a snack
- a special meal
- a special treat

What do you drink with these foods?

Get ready for PET Speaking Part 4

1 In Part 4 of the PET Speaking test, you have a conversation with your partner. You only have a few minutes for the task.
2 The examiner tells you what to talk about, but does not ask you any questions.
3 The topic of Part 4 is the same as the one in the pictures in Part 3.
4 Remember:
- talk to your partner, not to the examiner
- ask your partner questions
- listen and respond to what your partner says
- don't talk for too long, and give your partner a chance to speak.

1.20 3 **Look at the photographs again and listen to the examiner's instructions for the Part 4 task. What is the topic of the conversation? Make a list of the things you can talk about and the questions you can ask your partner. Think about how to begin the conversation.**

Have the conversation with another student.

1.21 4 **Listen to two students beginning the task. As you listen, think about:**

- how they begin
- how long each person speaks for
- how they show interest in what each other says

5 **Work with another student and do this Part 4 task. Don't talk for too long without involving your partner! Remember to ask questions and show interest. Use some of these phrases.**

Ask your partner questions.

Show interest in what your partner says.

That's interesting because …

I like …, don't you?

I agree with you about that.

Really?

So do I!

Me too, and another thing is …

What about you?

Talk together about good restaurants you have been to and what you like to eat there.

3 Vocabulary

1 Look at the recipe and picture. Can you complete the gaps in the list of ingredients?

some different-sized ....
a small tin of ....
two spoonfuls of ....
a hard-boiled ....
some black ....
two spoonfuls of ....

What equipment do you think you need to make this recipe?

1.22 **Now listen and check your ideas.**

1.23 **2 How do you think you make this recipe? Use these verbs and the ingredients above to talk about it.**

cut	mix	stir
pour	take out	

First you have to …

Then you …

Finally you …

Now listen and check your ideas. Complete the table as you listen.

	Equipment	Verb	Ingredients
1			
2			
3			
4			
5			
6			
7			

4 Writing

Complete the second sentence so that it means the same as the first, using no more than three words.

1 In our house, the salad is usually prepared by my brother.
In our house, my brother .... the salad.

2 At breakfast, all the orange juice was finished.
At breakfast, someone .... orange juice.

3 My mother said: 'Don't burn the rice!'
My mother told .... burn the rice.

4 In the restaurant, Robbie asked for a burger and chips.
In the restaurant, Robbie said: 'Can .... a burger and chips, please?'

5 Martine suggested we ordered a pizza.
Martine said: 'Let's .... a pizza.'

7 2

Your own space

1 Speaking

Talk about how important each of these things is for you at home:

1 a room or space which is your own
2 a quiet place where you can relax or study
3 a place where you can make as much noise as you like
4 a place where you can invite your friends in comfort
5 your own special seat at the dining table
6 somewhere outside, for example a balcony or garden

2 Reading

1 **Read this text about teenagers. Choose the correct word, A, B, C or D, for each space.**

PERSONAL SPACE

More and more people live in large cities these days and this means that it is becoming more and more difficult to find space and time for ourselves. But for many people, personal privacy is very important. In many homes, a few minutes in the bathroom is all the privacy that is **(1)** ....

Teenagers especially need their own personal space at home where they can feel relaxed and private. But, of course, not all teenagers are **(2)** .... enough to have a room of their own. Where space is short, they often have to **(3)** .... a bedroom with a brother or sister. In that case, it's a good **(4)** .... for them to have a special area or corner of the room to **(5)** .... their own. It's especially important for young people to have somewhere to **(6)** .... their personal things. This may or may not be a tidy place and it is not a good idea for parents to try and tell teenagers how to **(7)** .... their space as this is **(8)** .... to lead to arguments. Parents can, however, **(9)** .... sure that there are enough storage spaces such as shelves, cupboards and boxes. This will **(10)** .... the teenager to keep their space tidy if they want to.

	A	B	C	D
1	**A** confident	**B** available	**C** general	**D** average
2	**A** dizzy	**B** early	**C** lucky	**D** happy
3	**A** separate	**B** share	**C** divide	**D** join
4	**A** sense	**B** opinion	**C** idea	**D** thought
5	**A** mind	**B** call	**C** say	**D** tell
6	**A** belong	**B** save	**C** support	**D** keep
7	**A** organize	**B** repair	**C** operate	**D** review
8	**A** really	**B** quickly	**C** actually	**D** likely
9	**A** find	**B** make	**C** get	**D** put
10	**A** afford	**B** let	**C** allow	**D** set

2 **Read the complete text again and answer these questions.**

1 What is the writer trying to do in this text?
A complain about something
B blame someone for something
C give advice about something
D warn people about something

2 What does the writer believe?
A Teenagers can be selfish.
B Everybody needs some privacy.
C Parents can be unreasonable.
D Sharing is more important than privacy.

3 What does the writer think about tidiness?
A It is important for teenagers to be tidy.
B It is possible even when space is limited.
C It's a waste of time trying to be tidy.
D Parents should make their children be tidy.

3 Listening 1.24

Get ready for PET Listening Part 4

1 Part 4 of the PET Listening test is always a conversation between two people. They will be giving their opinions about something, and agreeing or disagreeing with each other.

2 Remember to read the instructions carefully to find out:
- who is talking
- where they are
- what they are talking about.

This will help you to imagine the situation and understand what they say.

3 Remember to read the sentences on the question paper carefully to:
- make sure you know whose opinion the sentence is about
- check if the sentence matches the text or not.

4 You may not understand all the words in the text. Don't worry, you only have to answer six questions with YES or NO. If you're not sure, guess. You have a 50 per cent chance of being right!

Read the questions carefully.

1 **Read the instructions for this Part 4 task.**
- Look at the six sentences for this part.
- You will hear a conversation between a man, Bob, and a woman, Mary. They are talking about their teenage children.
- Decide if you think each sentence is correct or incorrect.
- If you think it is correct, put a tick (✓) in the box under **A** for **YES**. If you think it is not correct, put a tick (✓) in the box under **B** for **NO**.

If you're not sure, then guess!

2 **Now listen and complete the task.**

		A YES	B NO
1	Mary's house is too small for Matthew to have his own room.	☐	☐
2	Matthew is a lot younger than his brother.	☐	☐
3	Bob wanted to spend more time alone as a teenager.	☐	☐
4	Matthew would like to have his own computer.	☐	☐
5	Mary feels that Matthew's brother has more need of a computer.	☐	☐
6	Matthew would like to watch the television more.	☐	☐

4 Speaking

What do you think?

1. How do you organize your personal space?
2. Do people respect your personal space?
3. Do you respect other people's space?
4. Do you think that tidiness is important?

5 Listening 1.25

Now do this task.

- Look at the six sentences.
- Alice and Harry are talking about their personal space.
- As you listen, decide if each sentence is correct or incorrect.
- If you think it is correct, put a tick (✓) in the box under **A** for **YES**. If you think it is not correct, put a tick (✓) in the box under **B** for **NO**.

		A YES	B NO
1	Alice regrets arguing with her mother.	☐	☐
2	Alice thinks her mother should put clothes away for her.	☐	☐
3	Alice tidies her room when she's expecting visitors.	☐	☐
4	Alice's wardrobe is too small for all her clothes.	☐	☐
5	Harry sometimes lets his brother wear his clothes.	☐	☐
6	Harry and his brother have to share a bedroom.	☐	☐

6 Speaking

Look at the two photographs. Talk about what you can see in each room.

A

B

8 1

Close to nature

1 Vocabulary

Use the words in the box to complete this text about the environment. Write one word in each space.

breathe	destroying	dusty	fuels	inhabitants	minerals
poverty	prevent	rescue	rubbish	spoil	urgent

STOP DAMAGING THE EARTH!

We have spent the last one hundred years **(1)** .... our environment. In cities, factories and cars pollute the air we **(2)** .... , and everything we touch is **(3)** .... and dirty. We **(4)** .... the countryside by throwing away our **(5)** .... there, and ruin areas of natural beauty by digging up **(6)** .... , such as iron and gold, and **(7)** .... , such as coal and oil. While some people get rich, others suffer from **(8)** .... , hunger and disease. We must **(9)** .... this situation from getting worse. Finding a way to **(10)** .... our planet is an extremely **(11)** .... problem for all the **(12)** .... of the world.

2 Listening 1.26

1 **Last Saturday three people went out for the day. They each took a photograph.**

A

B

C

Listen to the three people talking about the weather on their day out and decide which photo each person took.

Speaker 1 .... Speaker 2 .... Speaker 3 ....

2 **Listen to the three speakers again and write down all the weather words they use.**

Good weather	Bad weather	Other weather words
fine	*storms*	*forecast*

3 Speaking

Talk about:

- weather that makes you feel cheerful/depressed
- clothes you wear in different kinds of weather
- activities you do in different kinds of weather
- the weather and holidays, celebrations and sports events

4 Reading

Read the whole text first.

Read this text about gorillas. Choose the correct word, A, B, C or D, for each space.

THE GORILLA

The gorilla is a shy creature and seldom violent. In **(1)** ...., it is quite different from the dangerous animal we sometimes see in films and comic books. It only stands up on two legs and beats its chest if it wants to **(2)** .... an enemy away.

Gorillas are the largest and **(3)** .... powerful of all the apes. Adult males reach an average height of 150–170 cm and **(4)** .... from 135 to 230 kg. Females are smaller. **(5)** .... males and females are extremely strong and can tear down branches and pull up small trees. They **(6)** .... their days quietly in a leisurely **(7)** .... for food or resting in the warm sun.

Unfortunately, there are few of these animals **(8)** .... in the wild. This is mainly because people are cutting down the forests in **(9)** .... gorillas live. If we want to save the gorilla, we **(10)** .... take action now.

Try each word in the space before you choose the correct one.

	A	B	C	D
1	**A** fact	**B** case	**C** place	**D** turn
2	**A** throw	**B** go	**C** frighten	**D** run
3	**A** very	**B** much	**C** more	**D** most
4	**A** count	**B** weigh	**C** add	**D** measure
5	**A** Every	**B** Either	**C** Each	**D** Both
6	**A** spend	**B** use	**C** do	**D** make
7	**A** inquiry	**B** search	**C** study	**D** examination
8	**A** remained	**B** stayed	**C** left	**D** continued
9	**A** what	**B** which	**C** that	**D** where
10	**A** must	**B** ought	**C** may	**D** have

Get ready for PET Reading Part 5

1. First read through the whole text to get a good idea of the general meaning.
2. Sometimes your knowledge of *vocabulary* is tested, for example in 4. Only one of these verbs (*count*, *weigh*, *add*, *measure*) makes sense in this sentence. Try each word in the space before you decide which one is correct.
3. Sometimes your knowledge of *grammar* is tested, for example in 3. Only one of these words (*very*, *much*, *more*, *most*) is correct here. Which one? Why are the other words incorrect?
4. Sometimes your knowledge of *vocabulary and grammar* is tested, for example in 8. You could use the verb *remain* in this sentence, but, to be correct, you should write *remaining*, and not *remained*.

5 Listening

1.27 **You will hear an interview on the radio with Henry Tweedy, who is talking about his special dog, Lady. Put a tick [✔] against the correct answer for each question.**

1 Henry needs his dog because he can't
- **A** ☐ walk by himself.
- **B** ☐ see anything.
- **C** ☐ hear well.

2 Lady was chosen for training because
- **A** ☐ she was friendly and intelligent.
- **B** ☐ she already belonged to Henry.
- **C** ☐ she was a young dog.

3 What does Henry say about Lady's training programme?
- **A** ☐ It all happened in Henry's home.
- **B** ☐ It is still going on.
- **C** ☐ It took six months.

4 How does Lady communicate with Henry?
- **A** ☐ by running around
- **B** ☐ by touching him
- **C** ☐ by making a noise

5 When Henry wants Lady to do something, he
- **A** ☐ says certain words.
- **B** ☐ uses a hand signal.
- **C** ☐ gives her some food.

6 According to Henry, how does Lady feel about her work?
- **A** ☐ She loves being active and useful.
- **B** ☐ She would prefer to sleep more.
- **C** ☐ She finds new things hard to learn.

6 Speaking

Discuss these questions.

1 Someone wants to give you an animal as a pet. Which one will you choose? Why?

goldfish kitten duck rabbit mouse monkey

2 Which of these animals do you think helps humans most? Why?

bee chicken cow elephant horse dog

3 Which of these animals would you be most afraid to meet? Why?

spider snake shark bat tiger bear

7 Writing

This is part of a letter you receive from an English penfriend.

> I went horse-riding yesterday morning, and then I watched a brilliant TV programme about dolphins. I love all animals! How about you? Have you got a pet?

Now write a letter answering your penfriend's questions.
Write your letter in about 100 words.

8 2 The wide world

1 Reading

1 **Would you like to tour a foreign country on a bicycle? Which countries do you think it would be good to visit in this way? Would tourists enjoy travelling through your country by bike?**

2 **Read the sentences about cycling in Sri Lanka. Then read the text and decide if each sentence is correct or incorrect.**

1 More people in Sri Lanka ride a mountain bike than any other kind of bike.
2 The writer says that you can go a satisfactory distance each day on a bike.
3 The writer says a bicycle is a restful way of travelling through Sri Lanka.
4 The canals provide water for rice growing in spaces in the jungle.
5 The writer admired the colours of the countryside.

On two wheels in a green land

It is often said that the best way to see a country is to use the method of transport which is traditional in that particular place. So people should see Argentina on horseback, Nepal on foot and the US by car. If this is true, then a bicycle is the perfect way to visit Sri Lanka. Although the 18-speed mountain bike I used is not an everyday sight, more traditional models are popular all over the country.

Sharing the same kind of transport as local people changes the way you see the place. You are travelling at a speed that somehow fits the scenery – not so slow that you only see a small area each day, and not so fast that the details of the countryside are missed. Better still, you can stop whenever you want to listen to the birds or a waterfall, talk to people, smell their cooking or take a photo. However, this doesn't mean cycling in Sri Lanka is relaxing. If you want to see the whole country, you have to leave the towns and villages and cycle through jungle, where the temperature is 37 degrees, cross streams, climb hills and go over paths which are made of mud, rock or sand.

The most pleasant paths in the jungle follow the irrigation canals. These carry water into the bright green rice fields which appear at regular intervals among the trees. During the afternoon, groups of children, farm workers and water buffalo all come to swim in the canals. Then, when you climb from the jungle up into the hilly area in the centre of the country, you see every hillside is covered with neat rows of tea bushes in another brilliant shade of green. In fact, the whole country is covered in more different and beautiful shades of green than I ever thought possible.

Now I'm wondering where to ride my bike next – perhaps alongside the canals of The Netherlands, or through the city streets of China ...

2 Vocabulary

Look at these groups of words. Which one is different? Why?
Example:
sea ocean bush lake
***bush** is different because it's not water.*

1 mountain desert cliff hill
2 waterfall country continent district
3 forest wood jungle island
4 stream canal cave river
5 bay mud sand soil
6 path road track wave
7 valley coast shore beach
8 border flood frontier edge

3 Speaking

Do you like adventure films? What difficulties and dangers do the heroes meet? Who do you want to win in this kind of film – the heroes or the villains? Imagine this situation.

- A famous director of adventure films wants your advice about the location of his next film. Here are some places where the action in the film may happen.

- Talk about the adventures the hero and heroine may have in each place and say which you think will be the most exciting.
- Which actors would you like to star in this film? Do you think it would be a popular film?

4 Writing

Remember the second sentence must mean the same as the first one.
Write one, two or three words in each gap.

1 Here are some sentences about geography. Complete the second sentence so that it means the same as the first, using no more than three words.

1 Britain is an island, so everywhere is near to the sea.
Britain is an island, so nowhere is .... the sea.
2 Never walk in the desert without taking water with you.
Take water with you if you're .... a walk in the desert.
3 Look at a map of the Indian Ocean if you want to find Sri Lanka.
You won't find Sri Lanka unless .... a map of the Indian Ocean.
4 I became a geography teacher five years ago.
I .... a geography teacher for five years.
5 The geography teacher asked if they wanted to watch a video.
The geography teacher said, 'Would .... watch a video?'

Check what you have written carefully.

2 Now look at these sentences about going to live in a different country. Complete the second sentence so that it means the same as the first, using no more than three words.

1 Yesterday, our passport photos were taken by a photographer.
Yesterday, a photographer .... our passport photos.
2 My suitcases are heavier than my brother's.
My brother's suitcases aren't .... mine.
3 At first, we'll have difficulty understanding the language.
At first, understanding the language will be .... us.
4 We have to find a flat before we can look for a school.
We can't look for a school until we .... a flat.
5 My brother and I have both promised to send e-mails to our friends.
I've promised to send e-mails to my friends and .... my brother.

Get ready for PET Writing Part 1

1 This part is a test of your grammar. Everything you write must be correct.
2 The second sentence *must* have the same meaning as the first sentence.
3 There are several different kinds of changes that you have to make. For example:
- find words with the opposite meaning. (1.1)
- change the order of the words. (1.2)
- change the tense of the verb. (1.4)
- change reported speech to direct speech. (1.5)
- make a passive sentence into an active one. (2.1)
- change the way you compare two things. (2.2)

4 Remember you may have to write one, two or three words in your answer. Never write more than three words. Contractions (eg *don't*, *I've*) count as two words.

5 Reading

Look at the messages. What does each one say? Choose A, B or C.

1

To: Tyler
From: Liza

Can you record the programme about the world's oceans at 8.00 pm for me? I forgot to set the video before leaving home. Thanks.

A Liza wants to make sure she doesn't miss a television programme.
B Liza wants Tyler to get a video for them to watch this evening.
C Liza wants Tyler to stay at home until a television programme finishes.

2

To Class 6B
Your projects on Antarctica are due in on Monday. Still need help? Then try the websites on the list on the noticeboard.
Mrs Barton

A Mrs Barton will see students who need help with their projects on Monday.
B Mrs Barton would like students to help her with a website about Antarctica.
C Mrs Barton says websites may help students finish their work on time.

9 1 Free time

1 Vocabulary

1 **Rearrange these letters to make the names of sports.**
Example:
TALLBOFO = football

1 FRIWGUSNNID
2 BLATTNIESEN
3 FLOG
4 STYGNIMCAS
5 DOJU
6 COKYEH
7 SEALLABB

2 **Which of these sports do you like playing? What equipment do you need? Which of these sports do you like watching? What skills must the players have?**

2 Reading

What do you like to do in your school holidays?

- These people are all looking for a school holiday activity.
- Read the descriptions of eight school holiday activities on page 55.
- Decide which activity (letters **A–H**) would be most suitable for each person (numbers **1–5**).

1 Gwen is 18 and wants to take her younger brothers and sisters, aged between eight and 15, somewhere where they can get close to animals. She's just failed her driving test.

2 Matthew would like to take his daughter somewhere special on her sixth birthday, but he's only free in the afternoon. She loves hearing stories about animals but is frightened of real ones.

3 Lindsey has 11-year-old twin boys who hate sitting still. She wants to take them somewhere they can enjoy themselves safely all day while she goes to work.

4 Lewis is 15 and wants to do something exciting for the day with some friends from the school swimming team. They're keen to do something connected with either music or sport.

5 Jenny's going to look after her grandchildren, aged ten and seven, for the day. She can't afford to spend any money, but she'd like them to have some entertainment before she takes them home for lunch.

Holiday Fun for Young People

A Pineapple Theatre Every day at 3 o'clock, young children (4–7 years) can watch 'Stardog'. The fun dog from space invents things to help earth people. At 5 o'clock, a group of 10–16-year-olds presents 'Football Fever', a play about young sports stars. All tickets £3.

B Queen's Arts Centre A day-long course for children (9–13 years) introduces the art of telling stories through music and poetry. Use your own history to make a musical piece. Younger children (4–8 years) may use rubbish to make musical instruments and then play them. No charge for entrance.

C Museum Gardens Circus skills workshop for children (7–11 years). Try juggling, rope walking and putting on clown make-up. Or watch Tiptop Theatre tell the story of a Native American boy and his horse. Both programmes 10–12 am. Entrance free.

D Sunshine Safari We have three floors of slides, swings, rope bridges and other adventure activities. Young adventurers can join a tiger hunt or swim with crocodiles. It all seems very real! Leave your children (3–14 years) in the care of our trained staff. £35 per day, lunch extra.

E Balloon flight See the countryside without having to drive! Our gas-filled balloon is tied to the ground and doesn't actually travel, but the views are fantastic. Price: £12 adult, £7.50 child. No under 5s, no children under 16 without an adult.

F Sea Life Centre Discover facts about life under the sea and watch many varieties of fish. The three-hour tour includes handling starfish, feeding sharks and swimming with dolphins. Adults £4.95, children £3.50.

G Making waves This adventurous programme for 12–18-year-olds gives you a chance to try your skills in a sailing boat, a canoe and a motor boat for just £12 a day. Full instruction is given. You must be a good swimmer and agree to follow all safety rules.

H Paradise Animal Park Drive your car through the park and get close to some of the world's most beautiful and dangerous animals. Younger visitors can have fun in the play area, while there is excitement for older children in the adventure playground with its 10-metre free-fall slide. Family ticket £25.

Get ready for PET Reading paper

1 You have 1 hour and 30 minutes for the Reading and Writing paper. Plan your time carefully.
2 There are five reading parts to the paper. Each part has a different kind of reading text with its own questions.
3 You can get 35 marks for the Reading paper, one mark for each question.
4 In the exam you get a question paper and an answer sheet (see p.88). You can make notes on the question paper but you must mark all your answers on the answer sheet.
5 You must use pencil on the answer sheet. Take a pencil, pencil sharpener and rubber to the exam.
6 Read the texts carefully, but don't worry if there are words you don't understand. You probably don't need to know them to answer the questions.
7 Mark one letter for each question. To make a change, rub it out carefully and mark the new answer clearly.
8 If there is a question you can't answer, leave it and go back to it later.
9 Near the end of the test time, check your answers and make sure you have marked an answer for everything. If you don't know something, guess – you may be right!
10 There is more information about this paper in the **Get ready** boxes in this book. Make sure you read them again before the exam.

3 Vocabulary

1 **These people are all planning to do their favourite free-time activity. What does each person need? Choose the words from the box.**

I'm going to make a skirt to wear to the party tomorrow.

I'm going to decorate my bedroom and put up some shelves.

I'm going to answer this letter from my penfriend.

I'm going to do some work in the garden.

I'm going to have a game of tennis.

1 

2 3 

4 

5 

balls	brush	dictionary	envelope	flower pot	net
hammer	material	nails	needle	notepaper	
racket	paint	scissors	pins	watering can	
seeds	spade	sports bag	stamp	refreshing drink	

2 **What's your favourite free-time activity? What do you need to do it?**

4 Speaking

A friend of yours has just moved to a different town and wants to take up a hobby that will help him/her make new friends. Here are some pictures of some hobbies s/he could do.

- Talk about how interesting the different hobbies are, and decide which will be best for making friends.

9 2 Get well soon!

1 Writing

1 **Do you think you have a healthy lifestyle? What makes your lifestyle healthy or unhealthy?**

2 **You and your English friend, Alex, have decided to have a more healthy lifestyle.**
Write an e-mail to send to Alex. In your e-mail, you should

- tell Alex about your new sleeping habits
- say what type of food you plan to eat in future
- suggest some exercise or sport you can do together

Write 35–45 words.

2 Vocabulary

Read the sentences about health and sickness and find the missing words in the word square. They are written from top to bottom, left to right, right to left and diagonally.

1 This is an _ _ _ _ _ _ _ _ _ ! Some people have been hurt in a road _ _ _ _ _ _ _ _ , and they need an _ _ _ _ _ _ _ _ _ to take them to hospital.
2 I have bad _ _ _ _ _ _ _ so the doctor sent me to the ear _ _ _ _ _ _ at the hospital. Now I have to take a _ _ _ _ three times a day to make the _ _ _ _ go away.
3 A _ _ _ _ person can't hear without the help of a hearing aid.
4 A doctor and a _ _ _ _ _ both work in a hospital. A _ _ _ _ _ _ _ is a sick person they look after.
5 Even if we had a _ _ _ _ to cure every disease, would everyone be _ _ _ and healthy?
6 Doctor, I feel really _ _ _ . I've got a cold, a _ _ _ _ throat, and a high temperature. And just listen to my horrible _ _ _ _ _ ! I think I've got _ _ _ .
7 When I cut myself with a bread knife, the _ _ _ _ _ was quite deep. There was a lot of blood so my face went _ _ _ _ , I felt _ _ _ _ _ and thought I was going to fall over, but fortunately I didn't _ _ _ _ _.

A	M	B	U	L	A	N	C	E
C	L	I	N	I	C	U	P	M
C	S	E	H	C	A	R	A	E
I	O	Q	P	J	P	S	T	R
D	R	U	G	I	A	E	I	G
E	E	K	G	F	L	U	E	E
N	I	A	P	H	E	L	N	N
T	T	I	F	A	I	N	T	C
W	O	U	N	D	I	Z	Z	Y

3 Reading

Read the text and questions. For each question, decide which is the correct answer, A, B, C or D.

I'm sure I'm not the only person my age (15) who hates going to the dentist. Channel 4's late-night documentary *Open wide* last Tuesday was excellent for people like me. However, none of my school friends watched it. They missed this opportunity to see something interesting and educational because the programme didn't appear in the *TV Guide*. This was a pity, as it was the type of programme that makes both young people and their parents think about things they don't normally consider. Why can't television companies let us know about such important documentaries in advance?

This programme was important because it showed how methods for helping people with toothache have developed over the centuries. If you think visiting the dentist today is an uncomfortable experience, just be grateful you didn't live 200 years ago! Then, the programme told us, the only cure for toothache was removing the tooth. There weren't any dentists, so the person who cut your hair also pulled out your bad teeth, and there was nothing to stop you feeling the pain.

The programme has also completely changed my attitude to looking after my teeth. My parents were always saying to me things like, 'Don't eat too many sweets,' and, 'Brush your teeth after meals,' but I never paid much attention. Now I've seen what damage sugar can do, especially if I don't use a toothbrush regularly, I'm going to change my habits. Many people would benefit from a repeat of this programme. ”

Sophie Ashley, Oxford

1 Why has Sophie written this letter?
A to complain about the time a television programme was shown
B to ask for more television programmes designed for school children
C to advise people to watch a particular television programme
D to persuade a television company to show a programme again

2 Why didn't Sophie's school friends see *Open wide*?
A They didn't know it was on.
B They don't enjoy that type of programme.
C Their parents wouldn't let them.
D It wasn't shown on a channel they can receive.

3 What did *Open wide* say about toothache?
A In the past, nobody could make it stop.
B Dentists used to help people who had it.
C Hairdressers have it more than other people.
D Ways of curing it have changed.

4 What does Sophie think about her parents now?
A They don't know as much as her about teeth.
B Their advice is worth listening to.
C They eat things which are bad for them.
D They don't clean their teeth often enough.

5 Which of these gives information about the programme Sophie watched?

A A play about a 19th-century dentist and how he brought comfort to his patients.

B The series about health care for teenagers. This week, good eating habits.

C This history of the dentist's profession shows what happens when we eat.

D We suggest how to prepare young children for that first visit to the dentist.

4 Writing

Complete the second sentence so that it means the same as the first, using no more than three words.

1 Last night, I took an aspirin to stop my head aching.
Last night, I took an aspirin because .... aching.
2 My brother goes jogging because he must keep fit for his job.
My brother goes jogging to .... for his job.
3 If you don't give up coffee, you'll never sleep well.
You'll never sleep well unless .... coffee.
4 People with flu should stay in bed for a few days.
Stay in bed for a few days if you .... flu.
5 Smoking isn't allowed in hospitals.
You .... in hospitals.

5 Writing

Write one of the following questions.

1 **This is part of a letter you receive from an English penfriend.**

> I've got flu. I feel terrible and I'm bored because I have to stay in bed. What can I do to make myself feel more cheerful? Tell me about the last time you were ill.

Now write a letter answering your penfriend's questions.
Write your letter in about 100 words.

2 **Your English teacher has asked you to write a story.**
This is the title for your story:
The keep fit class

Write your story in about 100 words.

Get ready for PET Writing paper

1 You have 1 hour and 30 minutes for the Reading and Writing paper. The writing comes at the end of the paper, so plan your time carefully.
2 There are three writing parts to the paper: completing sentences, writing a short message and writing a letter or story.
3 You can get 25 marks for the Writing paper: 5 marks for Part 1, 5 marks for Part 2 and 15 marks for Part 3.
4 In the exam, you get a question paper and an answer sheet (see p.88–89). You can make notes on the question paper but you must write your answers on the answer sheet.
5 Write clearly. You don't want to lose marks because the examiner can't read your writing!
6 When you do Part 1, make sure that you don't write more than three words for any answer.
7 When you do Part 2, remember to write something about each point in the instructions.
8 When you do Part 3, try to make your letter or story clear and interesting.
9 Near the end of the test time, check your answers.
10 There is more information about this paper in the **Get ready** boxes in this book. Make sure you read them again before the exam.

10 1 Entertainment

1 Speaking

1 **How often do you do these things?**

watch television	sometimes
go to the cinema	quite often
surf the Internet	not very often
go to a concert	occasionally
go to the theatre	very often
go clubbing	never

2 **Match the things in this box with the different types of entertainment.**

curtain	encore	website	commercial
interval	soap opera	programme	backing group
ticket	channel	soloist	chat room

3 **Say what you like and dislike about each type of entertainment.**

2 Vocabulary

1 **Complete the text with words from the box. Use each word only once.**

part	clap	reviews	rehearsal	screen	camera
performance	series	director	stage	studio	lines

An actor speaks

As an actor, I much prefer working in the theatre to working on a film or a television **(1)** .... When I get a **(2)** .... in a play, I spend a long time learning my **(3)** .... and then there is a long period of **(4)** .... with the other actors before the first night. The good thing about a play, however, is that you are standing up on the **(5)** .... with a real live audience just a few metres away from you. At the end of the play, if they have enjoyed it, the people all **(6)** .... and you really feel good. It's interesting to read the **(7)** .... in the newspaper, but it's the people who are there who really matter.

Working in film or television, however, you spend too much time waiting in the **(8)** .... while the **(9)** .... crew make all the technical arrangements. You sometimes have to do the same bit over and over again until the **(10)** .... is satisfied with your **(11)** .... Then it is months or even years before the film or programme appears on the **(12)** .... By then, you've forgotten all about it and you're in the middle of doing the next thing, anyway.

2 **Choose the best answer, A, B, C or D.**

1 Why does the actor prefer working in the theatre?
A You have lots of time to practise.
B It's the same every night.
C There is a live audience.
D He always gets good reviews.

2 What does the actor dislike about working on films?
A It can be boring.
B You can get lonely.
C It is easy to forget your lines.
D You have to do two things at once.

3 **Fill in the missing word in these sentences.**

1 A .... is someone who writes in a magazine or newspaper.
2 A guitarist is someone who .... a guitar, often in a group.

4 **Make similar sentences to explain what these people do.**

drummer	director	photographer	TV presenter
disc jockey	comedian	pianist	film critic
interviewer	dancer	singer	violinist

3 Listening

1.28–30 1 **Listen to two friends discussing what to do this evening. Where do they decide to go?**

A ☐

B ☐

C ☐

2 **Listen to two friends talking about films. Which type of film do they decide to go and see?**

A ☐

B ☐

C ☐

3 **Listen to two friends discussing a film they have each seen. What did they like most about the film?**

A the plot
B the actors
C the camerawork

4 Speaking

Talk about a film, play or TV programme you have seen recently. Say what was good and bad about it. Remember to include information about the plot, camerawork and actors.

5 Listening 1.31

Get ready for PET Listening paper

1 You have about 30 minutes for the Listening paper.
2 There are four parts to the paper: Part 1 has seven short texts, and Parts 2, 3 and 4 have one long text each.
3 You can get 25 marks for the Listening paper, one for each question.
4 There are pauses between the listening texts. Make sure you use this time to read the questions for the next part, so you are ready to answer.
5 You hear each listening text twice. Answer the questions during the first listening. Check your answers when you hear the text for the second time.
6 In the exam you get a question paper and an answer sheet (see p.89). As you listen, write your answers on the question paper. At the end of the test, you have extra time to copy your answers on to the answer sheet.
7 You must use pencil on the answer sheet. Take a pencil, pencil sharpener and rubber to the exam.
8 Copy your answers carefully on to the answer sheet. Mark only one letter for each question. If you make a mistake, rub it out carefully and mark the new answer clearly.
9 Listen carefully, but don't worry if there are words you don't understand. You probably don't need to know them to answer the questions.
10 If there is a question you can't answer, just leave it and move on to the next one. You will probably hear the answer the second time you listen.
11 If you don't know the answer after the two listenings, guess – you may be right!
12 There is more information about this paper in the **Get ready** boxes in this book. Make sure you read them again before the exam.

Now try this listening task. Listen twice, as in the exam.

- Look at the notes about radio programmes.
- Some information is missing.
- You will hear an announcement about the programmes.
- For each question, fill in the missing information.

THIS MORNING'S RADIO

08.00	News
(1).......	*Arts Review* programme – information about theatre, concerts and films – special guest: Kevin Jones, **(2)** .... in a pop band.
08.45	**(3)** .... with Graham Smith.
08.50	New series: Polly Brown talks to people about **(4)** ....
09.30	**(5)** .... with James Grant.
10.15	Radio play called **(6)** '............'

6 Writing

Your English teacher has asked you to write a story.
Your story must begin with this sentence:

When the taxi came, Sandra was ready in her best dress and shoes.

Write your story in about 100 words.

The age of communication

1 Speaking

1 **Look at these ways of keeping in touch with people.**

letters	mobile phone	e-mail	fax	pager

Talk about:

- how often you use each one
- what you use each one for
- the good and bad things about each one

2 **Look at these two photographs. They both show people keeping in touch with their friends. Choose one of the photographs and talk about it. Remember to talk about all the things you can see, what the people are doing, and how you think they are feeling.**

A

B

Get ready for PET Speaking paper

1. You have 10–12 minutes for the Speaking paper.
2. You take the test with another student who is your partner. There are two examiners: one tells you what to do and the other one listens. Remember to speak clearly so both examiners can hear you.
3. There are four parts to the paper: talking about yourself, a situation, a photograph, and discussing a wider theme.
4. You can get 25 marks for the Speaking paper. You get marks for how well you communicate with your partner and for your pronunciation. There are also some marks for grammar and vocabulary.
5. Listen carefully to the examiner's instructions. If you are not sure what to do, ask the examiner to repeat them.
6. In Parts 2 and 4, talk to your partner – not to the examiner.
7. In Parts 2 and 3 the pictures are there to help you. Talk about what you can see and don't stop after you have talked about one thing. If you can't remember the word for something, don't worry. You can describe the thing or talk about something else.
8. Try to make the test easier for your partner and the examiner by being relaxed and friendly. In Parts 2 and 4, remember to ask your partner questions, show an interest in what they say, and give them a chance to speak.
9. There is more information about this paper in the **Get ready** boxes in this book. Make sure you read them again before the exam.

3 Practise this Part 2 task with a friend. Remember to talk about *all* the pictures, and don't decide too soon!

The examiner says:

I'm going to describe a situation to you. A friend is going away to study in another town. She will be living on her own in a student flat. She has some money to spend on one piece of electrical equipment, but she doesn't know what to buy. Talk together about the different things she can buy, and then say which will be best.

4 **Remember, you will be asked to spell your name in Part 1 of the test. Practise spelling these words out loud in English:**

- your first name
- your family name

2 Reading

Read the text below and choose the correct word, A, B, C or D, for each space.

THE RECIPE FOR GOOD COMMUNICATION

How many people do you communicate with in a day? Probably a lot more **(1)** .... you did ten years ago. With a few pieces of equipment, we can 'talk' to people in more and more ways, not **(2)** .... face-to-face and on the phone, but also via the Internet. It is very important, therefore, **(3)** .... everyone to try and improve their communication skills. Despite all the technological advances of **(4)** .... years, the art of good conversation is still at the heart of successful communication. **(5)** .... it's a good idea to remember the four golden rules of good communication. Firstly, be as clear as you can. Misunderstandings arise if we don't say exactly **(6)** .... we mean. Secondly, we have to work **(7)** .... at listening. Pay attention to what the other person is saying. Thirdly, ask **(8)** .... people what they think, don't only tell them what you think. And finally show respect for people, give them time to say what they want, and **(9)** .... interest in what they say.
If you **(10)** .... these rules, you will be a good communicator.

1	**A** like	**B** than	**C** as	**D** that
2	**A** yet	**B** even	**C** just	**D** still
3	**A** for	**B** if	**C** by	**D** from
4	**A** close	**B** last	**C** late	**D** recent
5	**A** There	**B** So	**C** Such	**D** Or
6	**A** when	**B** what	**C** which	**D** whom
7	**A** hard	**B** much	**C** great	**D** very
8	**A** every	**B** other	**C** each	**D** another
9	**A** get	**B** put	**C** be	**D** show
10	**A** act	**B** move	**C** follow	**D** go

3 Writing

Complete the second sentence so that it means the same as the first, using no more than three words.

1 My parents prefer using the telephone to using e-mail.
My parents think using the telephone is better .... e-mail.

2 My neighbour is confused by modern technology.
Modern technology .... my neighbour.

3 Whose is this mobile phone?
Who does this mobile phone .... to?

4 When I look at a screen for too long, I find it tiring.
I get .... when I look at a screen for too long.

5 Why don't you send Anne a text message?
If I were you, ... send Anne a text message.

PAPER 1 Reading and Writing Test 1 hour 30 minutes

READING

PART 1

Questions 1–5

Look at the text in each question.
What does it say?
Mark the correct letter **A**, **B** or **C** on your answer sheet.

Example:

0 **These animals are dangerous. Do not cross the safety fence.**

A Don't get any nearer to these animals because they may hurt you.

B Don't let these animals get out from behind this fence.

C It's dangerous to bring animals into this area.

Answer:

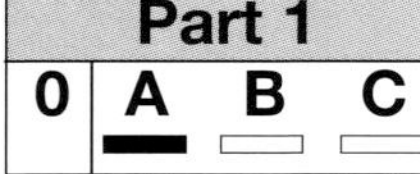
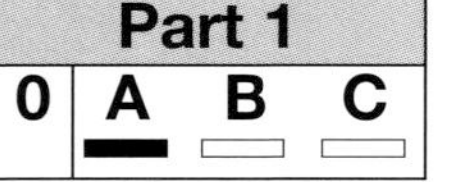

1 **Passengers' hand luggage must fit safely in the overhead lockers – if not, check it in**

A Passengers may take hand luggage unless it's too big for the overhead lockers.

B Passengers are not allowed to put any hand luggage in the overhead lockers.

C Passengers must close the overhead lockers after fitting in their hand luggage.

2

To: Mariella
From: Bruno

My washing machine's broken down again. Is it OK if I bring my washing round this evening? We can order pizza and have a chat.

A Bruno intends to mend his washing machine before ordering pizza for himself and Mariella.

B Bruno wants to help Mariella do her washing and make her pizza for dinner.

C Bruno is planning a pleasant evening at Mariella's while he does his washing there.

3

SAME-DAY DELIVERY
on all flowers ordered before 2 p.m.

A Order from us today and we will deliver your flowers by 2 p.m.

B If you place an order by 2 p.m., we can deliver your flowers today.

C Flowers are delivered at about 2 p.m. on the day after the order is made.

4

Tom
I'll be late this evening so can you record the football match? Then we can watch it together when I get home.
Dad

A Dad would like to go to a football match with Tom.

B Dad doesn't want Tom to watch the football match without him.

C Dad hopes to get home before the football match begins.

5

Please consider your neighbours and keep your music down after 11 p.m.

A Think of your neighbours and switch your music off at 11 p.m.

B Please play your music so your neighbours can hear it until 11 p.m.

C Your neighbours may want to sleep so don't play loud music later than 11 p.m.

PART 2

Questions 6–10

The people below all want to study English in Britain.
On the opposite page, there are descriptions of eight language schools.
Decide which language school would be the most suitable for the following people.
For questions **6–10**, mark the correct letter **(A–H)** on your answer sheet.

6 

Akiko, from Japan, is 19 and hoping to go to a British university to study fashion. First she'll spend a year at a language school in London improving her English and living with English people.

7 

Luiz Carlos is studying medicine in Brazil. He'd like to spend next February in any British city studying the kind of English that will help him in his future career. He'll find his own accommodation.

8 

Hanna is an English teacher from Poland. She's planning to spend August at a school somewhere outside London where she can do a teacher training course. She'd like accommodation to be provided.

9 

Yusuf, from the Ivory Coast, speaks almost no English and would like to study hard for six months to get a recognized qualification. He'll be happiest living outside London in a hostel with other students.

10 

Elena, from Spain, wants to bring her two daughters aged 9 and 11 to a school at the seaside for two weeks in July. It's important they enjoy themselves while improving their English.

ENGLISH SCHOOLS IN THE UNITED KINGDOM

A English Now
This school has just opened in London with the aim of providing English classes (30 hours per week) from July to September for students from other countries going to study at British universities. Students stay with English families or in a student hostel.

B Phillips Academy
This school in the Scottish capital of Edinburgh has courses for students who need to use English in their work. There are courses in English for business, for tourism, and for health service workers. Courses are available throughout the year. Rooms with local families can be arranged.

C Language Centre
This school is in a wonderful location on the coast four hours from London. There are classes for all ages (starting at age 8) between March and October (minimum stay one week). Teachers aim to make lessons fun and there are visits to places of interest in the afternoons. Accommodation is in guest houses.

D Walton College
This seaside school, 300 kilometres from London, offers course of either 2 or 4 weeks between June and September. Courses are for adults, for children aged 12 to 16, and for people wanting to improve their English teaching skills. There are trips organized every afternoon. Students live in single and shared rooms in the college.

E Drake English School
This school has branches in nine cities in the United Kingdom, but not London. Each branch offers classes (25 hours per week) for students at intermediate and advanced levels and provides special preparation for a number of recognized English exams. Students must register for at least one month. Accommodation is provided with English families.

F MPS Language Services
Situated in the centre of London, this language school offers year round courses (20 hours per week) at all levels for students aged 18 or over. Study advisers help with British university applications and work experience placements. Accommodation can be arranged with English families or in student hostels near the school.

G Turner House
This school in the northern city of Leeds offers a range of specialist advanced English courses, including English for business, for the hotel industry, and for doctors. There are also teacher training courses for experienced English teachers. Courses take place from April to November. Accommodation cannot be booked for students by the school.

H Dixon Hall
This school is situated in beautiful countryside three hours from London. There are classes (25 or 30 hours per week) at all levels from beginner to advanced. As students are encouraged to take one of a range of international exams, they usually stay from 3 to 12 months. Students stay in international student hostels.

PART 3

Questions 11–20

Look at the sentences below about a holiday on a cruise ship.
Read the text on the opposite page to decide if each sentence is correct or incorrect.
If it is correct, mark **A** on your answer sheet.
If it is not correct, mark **B** on your answer sheet.

11 A holiday on a cruise ship is suitable for children.

12 August is the most popular time to go on a cruise.

13 Staff on board will help parents by looking after their children while they play.

14 Passengers are encouraged to wear smart clothes at dinner time.

15 The ship's crew work as calmly behind closed doors as they do in public.

16 The ship's captain prefers to use technology as much as possible when sailing the ship.

17 If you book your cruise some time in advance, you may pay less.

18 It is difficult to find out how large your tips should be.

19 You are recommended to use e-mail rather than the satellite phone to contact people on land.

20 Being seasick on board is a common problem.

Holiday at Sea

My wife and I had never considered a cruise holiday because we have four children under fourteen and we didn't think a ship could offer the kind of facilities that kids enjoy. But we found we were wrong when we took a 9-day trip on the Caribbean Princess, a ship which can carry over three thousand passengers. We travelled last August, and so the ship was nearly full although more people go in July. We boarded the boat in Florida and our destinations were the Bahamas, Jamaica, the Cayman Islands and Mexico, which are all beautiful places to visit.

On board, my children had special clubs to go to so they always had plenty to do with people of their own age, while my wife and I could relax knowing professionals were keeping an eye on them. The on-board facilities were fantastic, including great shops, a jogging track, basketball courts and a range of excellent restaurants. Many people dress up for dinner and my family loved doing that but nobody makes you feel uncomfortable if you just wear ordinary clothes. After dinner, there's a choice of first class entertainment.

I wanted to find out what was involved in running such a big ship so I went through doors I wasn't really supposed to open! Out front, everything is calm and efficient, but behind the scenes there are people running around and working like mad. I was lucky enough to go on the bridge from where the captain sails the ship. There's an enormous amount of modern technology there but, being a real seaman, he likes to do as much as he can by hand.

I would definitely recommend a cruise holiday to anyone but make sure you search for the best possible price. You may get as much as a 45 per cent discount for an early booking. On the other hand, no cruise ship will leave half-empty so you might be able to get a last-minute, cheap ticket. Tipping is expected so save some money for that. Don't worry about what amount to give because you'll be told.

You'll want to keep in touch with people back home while you are away but remember that most mobile phones don't work at sea. You can make a satellite phone call from a cruise ship but that can cost as much as £9 per minute, so it's better to use the on-board e-mail service or wait until the next port to use a landline phone.

Unless you run into unusually bad weather, it is unlikely you'll be seasick. Most cruise ships are very large and specially designed so that they don't roll around in high seas.

PART 4

Questions 21–25

Read the text and questions below.
For each question, mark the correct letter **A**, **B**, **C** or **D** on your answer sheet.

Bertrand Piccard and his co-pilot Brian Jones were the first people to fly around the Earth in a balloon non-stop in 1999.

I learnt to fly in a balloon in a race across the Atlantic Ocean in 1992 and became fascinated by the sport. In the same way that a mountain climber dreams of climbing the world's highest mountain, I dreamed about flying non-stop around the world.

I spent six years planning the flight and failed twice before we managed to succeed. Our route took us over China, but we could only get permission to travel over the south. This meant going first to North Africa to catch the right winds. That added 10,000 kilometres, and another week, to our journey. But because of this, our flight broke all the records for distance and time spent in the air.

My main memory of the trip is that we lived in the air for 20 days and that the rising sun was the most amazing thing we saw. We had to go out of the balloon's capsule, in which we were transported, three times while in the air to repair the fuel system. We didn't have any safety equipment but when you are in a situation like that, you just do what you have to do without thinking about feeling afraid.

Landing was a fantastic moment. I remember that when I got out of the capsule, I looked at my footprint in the sand. I remembered the astronaut Neil Armstrong who was so happy to put his footprint on the moon, so far away from Earth. At that moment, I was so happy to have my foot back on Earth!

21 What is Bertrand Piccard's main reason for writing this text?
- **A** to compare the sport of ballooning with mountain climbing
- **B** to recommend ballooning as a means of transport
- **C** to describe the lessons that failure has taught him
- **D** to report on succeeding at something he'd dreamt of for years

22 Why did the balloon fly over south China?
- **A** The wind took it in the wrong direction.
- **B** The pilots weren't allowed to cross any other part.
- **C** The pilots were running out of time.
- **D** That route made the journey shorter.

23 Why did the pilots get out of the capsule during the flight?
- **A** to practise what to do in an emergency
- **B** to check the safety equipment was working
- **C** to mend something which had a fault
- **D** to test their courage in a dangerous situation

24 How does Piccard say he felt when he landed?
- **A** pleased to see a sign that he'd returned to Earth
- **B** proud to be told he was like Neil Armstrong
- **C** not able to stand or walk properly
- **D** like an astronaut returning from the moon

25 What was the newspaper headline after the balloon landed?
- **A** Balloon pilot flies alone around the world
- **B** Non-stop from North Africa to China
- **C** Magnificent record flight for Piccard and Jones
- **D** New record – 10,000 km in a week

PART 5

Questions 26–35

Read the text below and choose the correct word for each space.
For each question, mark the correct letter **A**, **B**, **C** or **D** on your answer sheet.

Example answer:

0	**A** near	**B** close	**C** about	**D** across

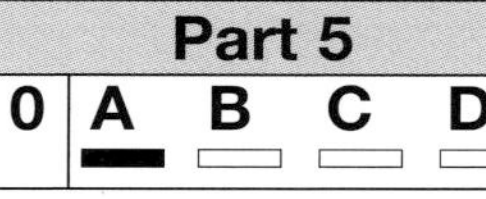

ISLAND FESTIVAL

Cheung Chau is a small island **(0)**...... Hong Kong in the South China Sea that has a colourful festival each spring. The main **(26)**...... of the festival is a procession through the streets in **(27)**...... children dressed in beautiful costumes are carried high in the air on long bamboo sticks. The children **(28)**...... to fly and the man who teaches them to do this is retired schoolteacher Yeung Yuk Lun. **(29)**...... child on the island hopes to be chosen to **(30)**...... part. 'Obviously, the children **(31)**...... to be small and light,' says Yeung Yuk Lun. 'This **(32)**...... they are usually between four and seven years old. They are extremely brave **(33)**...... it's quite frightening to be up in the air above a noisy crowd.' Towers of cakes are carried beside the children and offered to the ancient god Pak Tai, who, **(34)**...... to an old story, once **(35)**...... the island from great danger.

	A	B	C	D
26	**A** demonstration	**B** attraction	**C** invitation	**D** composition
27	**A** it	**B** this	**C** which	**D** what
28	**A** appear	**B** look	**C** play	**D** show
29	**A** Every	**B** All	**C** Most	**D** Many
30	**A** make	**B** do	**C** get	**D** take
31	**A** must	**B** should	**C** will	**D** have
32	**A** supposes	**B** aims	**C** means	**D** intends
33	**A** so	**B** because	**C** although	**D** unless
34	**A** opposite	**B** according	**C** up	**D** due
35	**A** saved	**B** provided	**C** covered	**D** supported

WRITING

PART 1

Questions 1–5

Here are some sentences about clocks and watches.
For each question, complete the second sentence so that it means the same as the first.
Use no more than three words.
Write only the missing words on your answer sheet.
You may use this page for any rough work.

Example:

0 Clocks and watches are seen everywhere.
You can ....*see*................. **clocks and watches everywhere.**

1 The earliest clocks used the sun's shadow to tell the time.
With the earliest clocks, people .... **the time by using the sun's shadow**.

2 Modern clocks are more accurate than old-fashioned ones were.
Old-fashioned clocks weren't as .... **modern ones are**.

3 The most famous clocks in the world are made in Switzerland.
In Switzerland, they .... **the most famous clocks in the world**.

4 An alarm clock can help you wake up early.
An alarm clock is helpful .... **you need to wake up early.**

5 People without watches are often late for appointments.
People without watches are often not .... **time for appointments**.

PART 2

Question 6

You have promised to take photos at your friend Sam's 18th birthday party next week, but now you can't go to the party.
Write an e-mail to Sam. In your e-mail, you should

- explain why you can't go to the party
- apologize
- suggest someone else who can take the photos.

Write **35–45 words** on your answer sheet.

PART 3

Write an answer to **one** of the questions (**7** or **8**) in this part.
Write your answer in about **100 words** on your answer sheet.
Put the question number in the box at the top of your answer sheet.

Question 7

- This is part of a letter you receive from an English penfriend.

I'm lucky because my school is really good and usually I love it. But some days I just hate it! What are the good and bad things about going to your school?

- Now write a letter answering your penfriend's question.
- Write your **letter** on your answer sheet.

Question 8

- Your English teacher has asked you to write a story.
- Your story must have this title:

  The message in the sand

- Write your **story** on your answer sheet.

PAPER 2 Listening Test 30 minutes (+ 6 minutes)

LISTENING

PART 1

Questions 1–7

There are seven questions in this part.
For each question there are three pictures and a short recording.
Choose the correct picture and put a tick (✓) in the box below it.

Example: Where did the man leave his sunglasses?

A ☐ B ☑ C ☐

1 What will the woman buy?

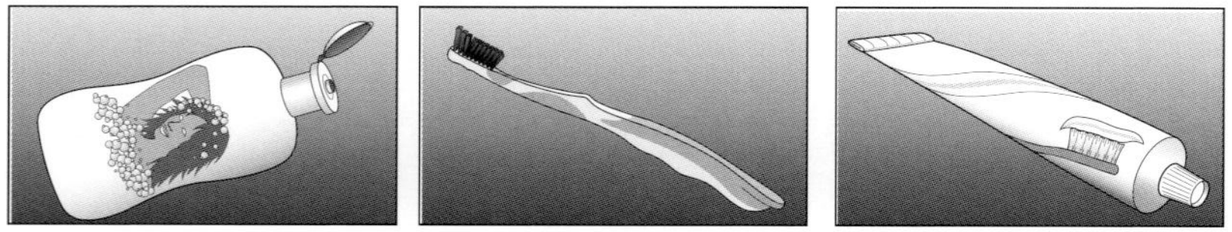

A ☐ B ☐ C ☐

2 Where is the woman's cookery book?

A ☐ B ☐ C ☐

3 What time will the next train for Bristol leave?

07:45 08:05 08:25

A ☐ B ☐ C ☐

4 Which yoghurt does the girl choose?

A ☐ B ☐ C ☐

5 Which band is the girl talking about?

A ☐ B ☐ C ☐

6 What did the boy get for his birthday?

A ☐ B ☐ C ☐

7 Which animal will be on the television programme first?

A ☐ B ☐ C ☐

PART 2

Questions 8–13

You will hear an interview with a woman who has written a popular novel.
For each question, put a tick (✓) in the correct box.

8 Anna's first novel was about
- **A** ☐ working in a school.
- **B** ☐ studying at a college.
- **C** ☐ learning to be a nurse.

9 How old was Anna when she got married?
- **A** ☐ 20 years old
- **B** ☐ 22 years old
- **C** ☐ 24 years old

10 An agent first liked Anna's story when
- **A** ☐ it was published in a magazine he read.
- **B** ☐ it won first prize in an Internet competition.
- **C** ☐ it was read out on a radio programme he heard.

11 What does Anna say about her new novel?
- **A** ☐ It is set in a place where she once lived.
- **B** ☐ It is about someone who is like her.
- **C** ☐ It is based on a family like hers.

12 What does Anna say about horses?
- **A** ☐ She would like to own one.
- **B** ☐ It would be fun to work with them.
- **C** ☐ Finding out about them was enjoyable.

13 Anna advises young writers to
- **A** ☐ wait until they have time to write properly.
- **B** ☐ keep writing even if it isn't going well.
- **C** ☐ spend all their free time writing.

PART 3

Questions 14–19

You will hear a student giving a talk about a person she admires.
For each question, fill in the missing information in the numbered space.

MICHAEL FOALE: SPACEMAN

Michael originally comes from **(14)** ....

Michael has spent a total of **(15)** .... in space.

Michael's first job was with a company that made **(16)** ....

Michael has to wear both a spacesuit and **(17)** .... when he walks in space.

In his most difficult space walk, Michael had to put a new **(18)** .... on a satellite.

Michael was surprised to find that the Moon is **(19)** .... in colour.

PART 4

Questions 20–25

Look at the six sentences for this part.
You will hear a conversation between a girl, Tanya, and a boy, Marek, about their holiday plans.
Decide if each sentence is correct or incorrect.
If it is correct, put a tick (✓) in the box under **A** for **YES**. If it is not correct, put a tick (✓) in the box under **B** for **NO**.

	A YES	B NO
20 Marek is pleased that he'll sleep in a tent on holiday.	☐	☐
21 Tanya and Marek both dislike travelling by air.	☐	☐
22 Tanya often regrets the things she buys at airports.	☐	☐
23 Tanya is going to a familiar place on holiday this year.	☐	☐
24 Marek thinks that Tanya's holiday sounds exciting.	☐	☐
25 Tanya will do some activities with her brother on holiday.	☐	☐

PAPER 3 Speaking Test about 12 minutes

PART 1 (2–3 minutes)

The test begins with a general conversation with the examiner, who will ask you and the other candidate some questions about yourselves. Be ready to talk about your daily life, your studies, your likes and dislikes, etc. In this part, you will be asked to spell all or part of your name.

PART 2 (2–3 minutes)

The examiner says:

In the next part, you are going to talk to each other. I'm going to describe a situation to you. Your teacher has invited the whole class to a party at her house. You would like to take her a present. Talk together about the types of present you could buy, and say which would be best.

See example visual on p. 75.

PART 3 (3 minutes)

The examiner says:

Now I'd like each of you to speak on your own about something. I'm going to give each of you a photograph of people eating. Please tell us what you can see in your

See example photographs on p. 76.

PART 4 (3 minutes)

The examiner says:

Your photographs showed people eating. Now I'd like you to talk together about things you like to eat in the winter and things you like to eat in the summer.

CANDIDATE MATERIAL – PART 2

CANDIDATE MATERIAL – PART 3

PAPER 1 Reading and Writing Test 1 hour 30 minutes

READING

PART 1

Questions 1–5

Look at the text in each question.
What does it say?
Mark the correct letter **A**, **B** or **C** on your answer sheet.

Example:

0

These animals are dangerous.
Do not cross the safety fence.

A Don't get any nearer to these animals because they may hurt you.

B Don't let these animals get out from behind this fence.

C It's dangerous to bring animals into this area.

Example answer:

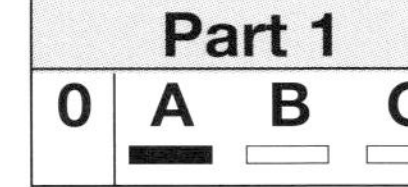

1

Wash dark colours separately at 40 °C. Dry flat away from direct sunlight.

A This mustn't be washed in water hotter than 40 °C or hung up to dry.

B This can safely be washed with white things and dried outside in the sun.

C This should be dry cleaned and not washed even at a temperature of 40 °C.

2

Karen,
This book is due back at the library today but if you want to read it, I'll get it out for another week.
Tracy

A Tracy is asking Karen if she can borrow her library book.

B Tracy is telling Karen to take her book back to the library.

C Tracy is offering to let Karen read her library book.

3

POST

My time spent studying Greek has been well worth it! Everyone here in this Greek village understands me although they often talk too fast for me to understand them!
Jessica

A Jessica is disappointed the Greek people can't understand her.

B Jessica feels she didn't spend enough time studying Greek.

C Jessica is pleased with her success in speaking Greek.

4

SALLY'S SANDWICHES
We're moving.
We'll welcome customers at 22 Canal Street from 7 June.

A We have already opened a new shop at a different address.

B You can't buy sandwiches in our new shop until 7 June.

C Customers will have to get their sandwiches from a different company after 7 June.

5

P PARKING
£2 per hour
3 hours maximum
£60 fine will be charged

A If you park here for 4 hours, you must pay a fine.

B It costs £60 to park here for 3 hours.

C Charges for parking go from £2 to £60.

PART 2

Questions 6–10

The people below are all making travel plans and want to visit the website of a travel company.
On the opposite page, there are descriptions of eight travel company websites.
Decide which website would be the most suitable for the following people.
For questions **6–10**, mark the correct letter **(A–H)** on your answer sheet.

6 Guy is a student who is planning a long trip alone through South America next year. He wants to find out more about the area, and about how he can save money, before booking anything.

7 Lenka wants to book a holiday for herself, her husband and four children on the Mediterranean coast of France. She wants to stay in a flat and hire a car.

8 Nikil has to book accommodation for 12 work colleagues who are going to London next month. He wants to use a company that has been in business for some time which will give a discount.

9 Sonia has already booked her skiing holiday in the Swiss Alps. She now needs to buy skis and boots to take with her.

10 Daniel wants to surprise his wife with tickets for a voyage on a Caribbean cruise ship. He doesn't have too much money to spend and they have to go in the next few days.

Travel Company Websites

A Best Choice

Whether you plan to travel to Europe, Asia, Africa, Australia or the Americas, we have what you need. We sell a wide range of clothing for children and adults to wear in the sun or snow, plus travel bags and all the equipment necessary for your winter sports or scuba diving holiday.

B LTC Travel

Our website is the first stop for all young, independent travellers. We give advice on travel to all parts of North and South America, including the Caribbean, and direct you towards cheap flights and low-priced accommodation. You can download free maps and country guides.

C Swift Holidays

We promise to get you the cheapest flight available to your chosen destination. We can also find you many kinds of holiday at a reduced cost if you book at the last minute. This week's special offers include a skiing holiday in the Swiss Alps and a cruise in the Caribbean.

D Go-With-Us

If you want to give your family the holiday of a lifetime, let us take care of you. Choose from a number of campsites in seaside and mountain locations throughout Europe. The price includes travel, use of a luxury tent, first-class campsite facilities, organized sporting activities and evening entertainment.

E Easy Journey

We can take the worry out of making holiday reservations. We organize group holidays (minimum size six) to a range of beautiful seaside locations around the Mediterranean and Caribbean Seas. Every sixth person in the group goes free. Stay in a three-star hotel or a holiday apartment. Car-rental included in the price.

F Faraway Tours

We offer discounts on plane fares to Asia and the Far East to students and anyone under 26. We also supply camping, mountain-climbing and sailing clothes and equipment. Travellers can exchange information, opinions and experiences in an online chat room.

G Take Off

We are a new company whose aim is to make business travel trouble-free and enjoyable. We can arrange first class tickets to anywhere in the world at a moment's notice and also make bookings at hotels with business and conference facilities. Our prices can't be beaten.

H Globetrotter

We have made travel arrangements to worldwide destinations for thirty years. We also book hotel rooms and organize car hire in all European and North American cities. We only deal with well-respected tour operators so you can be confident about our service. There are reduced prices for group bookings.

PART 3

Questions 11–20

Look at the sentences below about a school of theatre arts.
Read the text on the opposite page to decide if each sentence is correct or incorrect.
If it is correct, mark **A** on your answer sheet.
If it is not correct, mark **B** on your answer sheet.

11 Students are sometimes taught by people from outside who are employed in the theatre.

12 Students can still get support from the school when they have finished their course.

13 At their interview, acting course candidates have to perform more than musical theatre candidates.

14 It usually takes more than two weeks before candidates hear the decision of the interviewers.

15 All students on the full-time course study the same things.

16 The full-time course is designed to qualify students for many kinds of work in the profession.

17 From the start of the 'Acting for the screen' course, students take part in films.

18 If you are 15 and want to act, you could study at the school in July.

19 It's better if young people already have some performing skills before doing the musical theatre course.

20 Applications for part-time courses should be made in the four weeks before the course begins.

Welcome to the Gordon Lake School of Theatre Arts

The Gordon Lake School is one of the country's leading drama schools, offering both full-time and part-time courses for those interested in a career in acting, musical theatre, directing or technical theatre.

Our permanent teaching staff are dedicated professionals who want each individual student to develop his or her skills and abilities to the full. Students also work with visiting staff who are currently earning their living in theatre, film and television.

The Gordon Lake School continues to advise students even after they have completed their studies. We run our own theatrical agency to help you find work in the profession.

Before entering the school

After we have received your application form, we will invite you to an interview and ask you to perform for us. Candidates wanting to take the acting course will have to learn and perform two pieces taken from plays. Candidates who would like to study musical theatre are required to sing two songs and take part in a dance workshop in addition to doing the two pieces from plays. Candidates are normally informed whether or not they will be offered a place on a course within two weeks of the interview.

Full-time course

After successfully completing three years of study, students receive a BA degree in performance arts. Students will be able to choose from a range of course options, depending on whether they want to concentrate on acting, musical theatre, directing or technical theatre. See our brochure for full details of these options. The aim behind all course options is to produce professionals with the ability to be regularly employed in a very varied industry.

Part-time courses

The school also offers a range of evening, weekend and summer courses for people of all ages and backgrounds These include the following:

- **Acting for the screen:** This is a two-term course on Monday evenings from 7 to 10 p.m. The first term concentrates on developing screen-acting techniques. The second term builds on this knowledge in the making of a series of short films.
- **Acting course for young people:** This five-day summer course is held every July for young people aged 12–18 who are thinking of an acting career.
- **Musical theatre course for young people:** This course is on Saturday afternoons throughout January, February and March. It is designed to train young people (11–18 years) in professional song and dance techniques. Some previous experience of dance and singing is preferred and a keen interest in performing is essential.

Applications for all part-time courses must be with us at least a month before term begins. Late applications may be considered if spaces are available.

PART 4

Questions 21–25

Read the text and questions below.
For each question, mark the correct letter **A**, **B**, **C** or **D** on your answer sheet.

Polly Murray, explorer

In a way, I've been an explorer all my life. My earliest memory is of a family camping holiday in Italy when I was six. We put up our tent at 4,000 metres! I remember walking down the mountain, holding my father's trousers to prevent me from falling over the rock edge. I didn't have any fear of heights then. Now I rather like looking down and feeling a bit afraid.

I spend every winter in the mountains teaching skiing. The rest of the time I go exploring. This year, I've tested out an adventure holiday in Patagonia in Argentina for a travel company and helped a TV company make a nature film in the jungle in Peru. My most exciting trip has been one I took with my friend Tania. We sailed from Greenland across Baffin Bay to Bylot Island, which is just ice, mountains and polar bears. We crossed the island on foot in seven days but, when we got to the other side, the boat wasn't there to meet us as planned. There was a terrific storm and it couldn't get to the shore, which meant we had to wait two extra days. We had run out of food and were very hungry, and very nervous about the polar bears.

To be an explorer, you need to be cool-headed. The minute you start to panic everything goes wrong, especially if you're climbing. I haven't had any serious accidents or injuries although I once had terrible toothache in Antarctica in the middle of nowhere. I just had to carry on in spite of the pain. I think I am a strong person and I can't imagine having any other kind of life.

21 What is Polly's main reason for writing this text?
A to advertise exciting holidays
B to recommend climbing as a sport
C to describe her way of life
D to encourage people to travel

22 What happened to Polly at the age of six?
A She went camping in the mountains.
B She fell when she was mountain climbing.
C She became frightened of high mountains.
D She and her father got lost in the mountains.

23 Polly couldn't leave Bylot Island when she wanted to because
A polar bears stopped her from crossing the ice.
B she was too weak and hungry to travel.
C she was waiting in the wrong place for her boat.
D bad weather prevented her boat from reaching her.

24 According to Polly, a good explorer is someone who
A avoids accidents and injuries.
B learns from bad experiences.
C is able to climb difficult mountains.
D can stay calm in any situation.

25 Which person is talking about Polly?

A A travel company sent us to Peru together to see what we thought of an adventure holiday there.

B She's a great ski instructor but I don't understand how she can enjoy feeling frightened of heights.

C She had bad toothache once when she was on a trip and had to come home.

D Exploring is fine when you're young but now she's older she's thinking about giving it up.

PART 5

Questions 26–35

Read the text below and choose the correct word for each space.
For each question, mark the correct letter **A**, **B**, **C** or **D** on your answer sheet.

Example:

0	**A** results	**B** decisions	**C** effects	**D** events

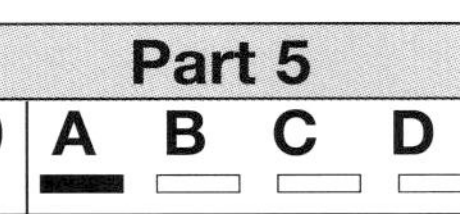

WOMEN MAKE THE BEST DRIVERS

In London, only one in ten bus drivers is a women. Yet, according to the **(0)**...... of recent research, women are better at **(26)**...... with problem passengers, have fewer accidents and are quicker at learning to drive buses than men.

Connie Wilson **(27)**...... a bus driver a year ago. '**(28)**...... first, driving a bus was quite frightening,' she says. 'I had no idea of the size of the vehicle or **(29)**...... to handle it. But after seven weeks of training, I passed the test first time. Trying to **(30)**...... to the timetable when the traffic is **(31)**...... isn't easy but I like the challenge! Some passengers **(32)**...... be rude, especially if they've had to **(33)**...... a long time for the bus. But most are pleased to have a woman driver. There's no **(34)**...... why women can't do the job just as well as men. I'd **(35)**...... it to any woman.'

26	**A** managing	**B** dealing	**C** considering	**D** behaving
27	**A** got	**B** started	**C** turned	**D** became
28	**A** At	**B** By	**C** In	**D** From
29	**A** what	**B** which	**C** why	**D** how
30	**A** check	**B** respect	**C** keep	**D** carry
31	**A** deep	**B** large	**C** heavy	**D** rough
32	**A** can	**B** should	**C** need	**D** want
33	**A** delay	**B** wait	**C** expect	**D** attend
34	**A** cause	**B** reason	**C** purpose	**D** account
35	**A** approve	**B** lead	**C** recommend	**D** admire

WRITING

PART 1

Questions 1–5

Here are some sentences about the alphabet.
For each question, complete the second sentence so that it means the same as the first.
Use no more than three words.
Write only the missing words on your answer sheet.
You may use this page for any rough work.

Example: The alphabet we use in English has 26 letters.
In the alphabet we use in English, ...*there*.................. **are 26 letters.**

1 The two Greek letters 'alpha' and 'beta' give us the word 'alphabet'.
We get the word 'alphabet' .... **the two Greek letters 'alpha' and 'beta'.**

2 An alphabet was first used about 3,500 years ago.
People .... **an alphabet for about 3,500 years.**

3 Without an alphabet, we couldn't write down our ideas.
If we .... **have an alphabet, we couldn't write down our ideas.**

4 You can't learn to read and write until you know your alphabet.
You must know your alphabet .... **you can learn to read and write.**

5 Is learning the alphabet easier for children than learning to count?
Is learning to count not .... **for children as learning the alphabet?**

PART 2

Question 6

An English family has moved into the apartment next door to you, and you'd like to introduce yourself to them.
Write a note to the family. In your note, you should

- introduce yourself
- give them a piece of useful information about the neighbourhood
- offer to do something for the family.

Write **35–45 words** on your answer sheet.

PART 3

Write an answer to **one** of the questions (**7** or **8**) in this part.
Write your answer in about **100 words** on your answer sheet.
Mark the question number in the box at the top of your answer sheet.

Question 7

- This is part of a letter you receive from an English penfriend.

> *I'm planning to visit your country soon. Where should I go? I'm interested in history, beautiful scenery and anything you recommend.*

- Now write a letter to tell your penfriend about places to visit in your country.
- Write your **letter** on your answer sheet.

Question 8

- Your English teacher has asked you to write a story.
- Your story must begin with this sentence:

  Emma didn't know how to find the money she needed.

- Write your **story** on your answer sheet.

PAPER 2 Listening Test 30 minutes (+ 6 minutes)

LISTENING

PART 1

Questions 1–7

There are seven questions in this part.
For each question there are three pictures and a short recording.
Choose the correct picture and put a tick (✓) in the box below it.

Example: Where did the man leave his sunglasses?

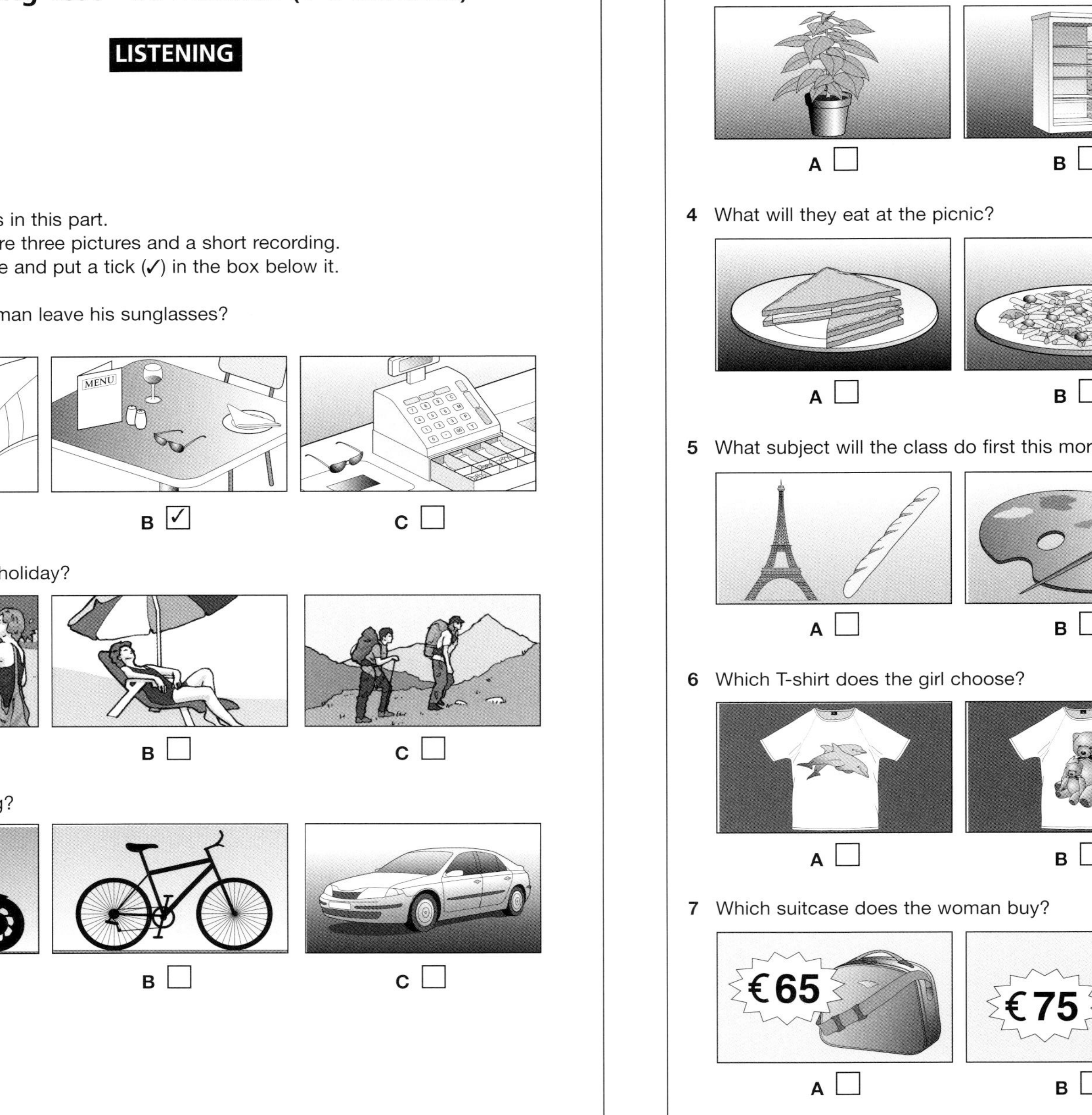

A ☐ B ☑ C ☐

1 Where will they go on holiday?

A ☐ B ☐ C ☐

2 What are they cleaning?

A ☐ B ☐ C ☐

3 Where's the water coming from?

A ☐ B ☐ C ☐

4 What will they eat at the picnic?

A ☐ B ☐ C ☐

5 What subject will the class do first this morning?

A ☐ B ☐ C ☐

6 Which T-shirt does the girl choose?

A ☐ B ☐ C ☐

7 Which suitcase does the woman buy?

A ☐ B ☐ C ☐

PART 2

Questions 8–13

You will hear an interview with Stella Brady who is a professional photographer.
For each question, put a tick (✓) in the correct box.

8 Stella first won a photography competition when she was

A ☐ eight years old.
B ☐ ten years old.
C ☐ twelve years old.

9 Stella first learnt about photography from

A ☐ her parents.
B ☐ her uncle.
C ☐ her brother.

10 What did Stella do when she left school?

A ☐ She got a job to make some money.
B ☐ She went on holiday before starting work.
C ☐ She did some training in photography.

11 What does Stella say about Australia?

A ☐ She didn't enjoy taking photos there.
B ☐ She learnt a lot about photography there.
C ☐ She found lots of work as a photographer there.

12 In Stella's studio, you can mostly see

A ☐ photos of weddings.
B ☐ sports photography.
C ☐ artistic photographs.

13 In the future, Stella plans to

A ☐ try a new kind of photography.
B ☐ take photographs of works of art.
C ☐ start painting people instead.

PART 3

Questions 14-19

You will hear a tour guide talking to some visitors in a jewellery workshop.
For each question, fill in the missing information in the numbered space.

JEWELLERY WORKSHOP

Where many of the artists come from:	**(14)** ....
The metal they use most:	**(15)** ....
What they use instead of stones:	**(16)** .... *or seeds*
What the artist thinks of first:	*the* **(17)** .... *of the piece*
Where many of the artists get their ideas:	*from* **(18)** ....
Where people wear the workshop's best-known jewellery:	*in their* **(19)** ....

PART 4

Questions 20–25

Look at the six sentences for this part.
You will hear a conversation between a boy, Darren, and a girl, Monica, about a football match.
Decide if each sentence is correct or incorrect.
If it is correct, put a tick (✓) in the box under **A** for **YES**. If it is not correct, put a tick (✓) in the box under **B** for **NO**.

	A YES	B NO
20 Monica remembers seeing Darren at the football match.	☐	☐
21 Monica admits this was the first match she's ever been to.	☐	☐
22 Monica's friends were surprised by the size of the stadium.	☐	☐
23 Darren and Monica agree that going to a match is expensive.	☐	☐
24 Monica was disappointed by the match itself.	☐	☐
25 Darren thinks that the local team played well enough to win.	☐	☐

PAPER 3 Speaking Test about 12 minutes

PART 1 (2–3 minutes)

The test begins with a general conversation with the examiner, who will ask you and the other candidate some questions about yourselves. Be ready to talk about your daily life, your studies, your likes and dislikes, etc. In this part, you will be asked to spell all or part of your name.

PART 2 (2–3 minutes)

The examiner says:

In the next part you will talk to each other. I'm going to describe a situation to you. A group of teenagers from Australia is coming to spend a week in this country in the spring. They have asked what things they need to bring with them. Talk together about the different things they should bring and say which will be the most useful.

See example visual on p. 86.

PART 3 (3 minutes)

The examiner says:

Now I'd like each of you to talk on your own about something. I'm going to give each of you a photograph of people studying. Please tell us what you can see in your photograph.

See example photographs on p. 87.

PART 4 (3 minutes)

The examiner says:

Your photographs showed people studying. Now I'd like you to talk together about where you go when you want to study, and the best time of day for studying.

CANDIDATE MATERIAL – PART 2

READING AND WRITING – ANSWER SHEET 1

UNIVERSITY *of* CAMBRIDGE
ESOL Examinations

Candidate Name
If not already printed, write name in CAPITALS and complete the Candidate No. grid (in pencil).

Candidate Signature

Examination Title

Centre

Supervisor:
If the candidate is ABSENT or has WITHDRAWN shade here

Centre No.

Candidate No.

Examination Details

0	0	0	0
1	1	1	1
2	2	2	2
3	3	3	3
4	4	4	4
5	5	5	5
6	6	6	6
7	7	7	7
8	8	8	8
9	9	9	9

PET Paper 1 Reading and Writing Candidate Answer Sheet 1

Instructions

Use a PENCIL (B or HB).

Rub out any answer you want to change with an eraser.

For Reading:

Mark ONE letter for each question.
For example, if you think **A** is the right answer to the question, mark your answer sheet like this:

0	A	B	C	D

Part 1	
1	A B C
2	A B C
3	A B C
4	A B C
5	A B C

Part 2	
6	A B C D E F G H
7	A B C D E F G H
8	A B C D E F G H
9	A B C D E F G H
10	A B C D E F G H

Part 3	
11	A B
12	A B
13	A B
14	A B
15	A B
16	A B
17	A B
18	A B
19	A B
20	A B

Part 4	
21	A B C D
22	A B C D
23	A B C D
24	A B C D
25	A B C D

Part 5	
26	A B C D
27	A B C D
28	A B C D
29	A B C D
30	A B C D
31	A B C D
32	A B C D
33	A B C D
34	A B C D
35	A B C D

Continue on the other side of this sheet →

PET RW 1 DP491/389

READING AND WRITING – ANSWER SHEET 1 (REVERSE)

For Writing (Parts 1 and 2):

Write your answers clearly in the spaces provided.

Part 1: Write your answers below.	Do not write here
1	1 1 0
2	1 2 0
3	1 3 0
4	1 4 0
5	1 5 0

Part 2 (Question 6): Write your answer below.

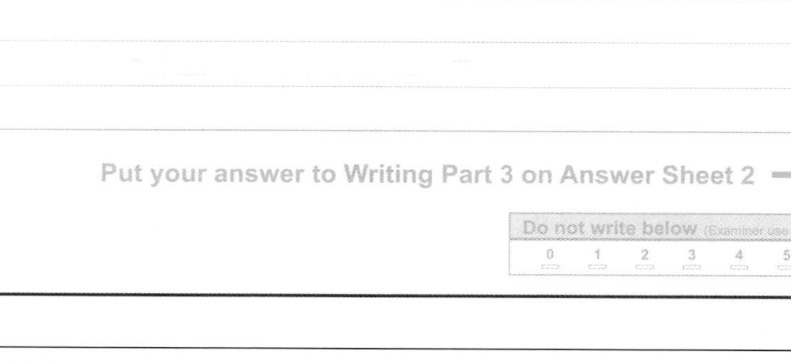

Put your answer to Writing Part 3 on Answer Sheet 2 →

Do not write below (Examiner use only)					
0	1	2	3	4	5

READING AND WRITING – ANSWER SHEET 2

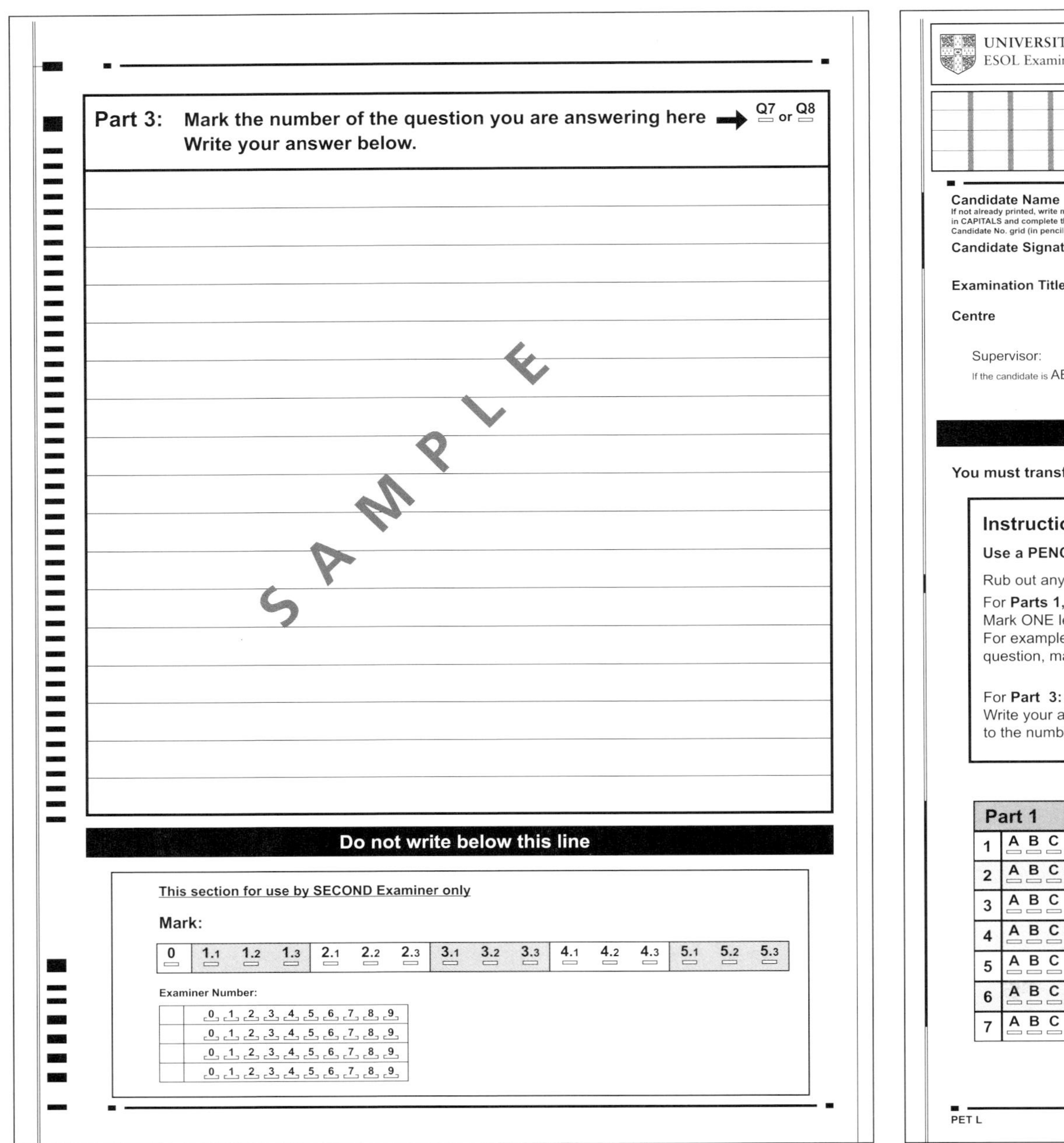

Part 3: Mark the number of the question you are answering here → Q7 or Q8
Write your answer below.

Do not write below this line

This section for use by SECOND Examiner only

Mark:

0	1.1	1.2	1.3	2.1	2.2	2.3	3.1	3.2	3.3	4.1	4.2	4.3	5.1	5.2	5.3

Examiner Number:

	0	1	2	3	4	5	6	7	8	9
	0	1	2	3	4	5	6	7	8	9
	0	1	2	3	4	5	6	7	8	9
	0	1	2	3	4	5	6	7	8	9

LISTENING – ANSWER SHEET

UNIVERSITY *of* CAMBRIDGE
ESOL Examinations

Candidate Name
If not already printed, write name in CAPITALS and complete the Candidate No. grid (in pencil).

Candidate Signature

Examination Title

Centre

Supervisor:
If the candidate is ABSENT or has WITHDRAWN shade here

Centre No.

Candidate No.

Examination Details

0	0	0	0
1	1	1	1
2	2	2	2
3	3	3	3
4	4	4	4
5	5	5	5
6	6	6	6
7	7	7	7
8	8	8	8
9	9	9	9

PET Paper 2 Listening Candidate Answer Sheet

You must transfer all your answers from the Listening Question Paper to this answer sheet.

Instructions

Use a PENCIL (B or HB).

Rub out any answer you want to change with an eraser.

For **Parts 1, 2** and **4:**
Mark ONE letter for each question.
For example, if you think **A** is the right answer to the question, mark your answer sheet like this:

0	A B C

For **Part 3:**
Write your answers clearly in the spaces next to the numbers (14 to 19) like this:

0	example

Part 1		Part 2		Part 3		Do not write here	Part 4	
1	A B C	8	A B C	14		1 14 0	20	A B
2	A B C	9	A B C	15		1 15 0	21	A B
3	A B C	10	A B C	16		1 16 0	22	A B
4	A B C	11	A B C	17		1 17 0	23	A B
5	A B C	12	A B C	18		1 18 0	24	A B
6	A B C	13	A B C	19		1 19 0	25	A B
7	A B C							

PET L

DP493/391

Grammar and vocabulary practice

Unit 1

Grammar

1 Complete the text with the correct prepositions.

Every morning when I wake **(1)** .... , I turn **(2)** .... the light next to my bed to see what time it is. I don't like getting **(3)** .... any earlier than I need to, so I set the alarm in my mobile phone to go **(4)** .... at seven o'clock, but I'm usually awake before that.

I usually wait to see what the weather is like before deciding what clothes to put **(5)** .... So I switch **(6)** .... the radio while I'm in the bathroom and listen **(7)** .... for the weather forecast.

Vocabulary

2 How many words can you find in the wordsquare? Complete the sentences with the words you find.

Across

1 You put one .... on each foot.
2 You use a .... to correct a mistake.
3 A .... is a quick way of washing yourself.
4 A .... helps you draw a straight line.
5 A .... is useful for putting books on.
6 You dry yourself with a ....
7 You use a .... to keep your hair tidy.
8 You use .... when you wash your hands.

Down

1 You clean your teeth with a ....
2 .... are useful for cutting paper.
3 You wear a .... so that you always know the time.
4 A .... goes under you in bed.
5 A .... is useful for writing notes.
6 A .... helps you to read in bed.
7 You might get a lift to school in a ....
8 You probably use .... when you wash your hair.

C	O	M	B	T	O	W	E	L
C	S	I	S	O	A	P	O	A
S	W	S	H	O	W	E	R	M
C	A	H	E	T	Z	N	F	P
I	T	A	E	H	B	C	N	C
S	C	M	T	B	C	I	M	A
S	H	P	W	R	U	L	E	R
O	G	O	R	U	B	B	E	R
R	X	O	P	S	H	E	L	F
S	O	C	K	H	F	G	U	Q

Unit 2

Vocabulary

1 Choose the correct word(s).

1 You go to a *library/bookshop* to buy a book.
2 A *romance/novel* is a book about a love affair.
3 You need a lot of *fantasy/imagination* to be a writer.
4 Jon was *educated/brought up* at a university in Paris.
5 Sally *met/knew* lots of new people on her first day at college.
6 Have you *made/done* your homework yet?
7 How *much/many* does this book cost, please?

Grammar

2 Complete the sentences with the correct prepositions.

1 .... my opinion, this book is too long.
2 I agree .... you about that novel. It's brilliant.
3 I lent that book .... my brother.
4 You can depend .... the information in that book. It's all accurate.
5 Tom logged .... to a website in English to help him with his homework.

Unit 3

Grammar

1 Choose the correct word(s).

1 I can't go out this evening, I've got *too much/too many* homework to do.
2 He's got a good job and earns *many/a lot of* money.
3 I'm *too/too much* tired to walk any further.
4 I haven't got *enough/too* money to go away on holiday this year.
5 He's a *too/very* lucky man because he gets free flights all over the world.

Vocabulary

2 Match the jobs in A with the places of work in B.

A

pilot	dentist	hairdresser	judge
lecturer	engineer	secretary	sales assistant
waiter	presenter	nurse	footballer
priest	fisherman	farmer	

B

hospital	aeroplane	church	restaurant
TV station	stadium	surgery	shop
farm	college	salon	office
factory	court	ship	

3 In which of the jobs in A would you use:

1 a comb?
2 a tray?
3 a thermometer?
4 a net?
5 an envelope?
6 a microphone?
7 a tractor?
8 a pair of shorts?

Unit 4

Vocabulary

1 **Match (1–15) to (a–o) to make the names of household objects.**

1 air	**a** player
2 alarm	**b** washer
3 arm	**c** basket
4 book	**d** conditioning
5 central	**e** machine
6 dish	**f** oven
7 DVD	**g** clock
8 frying	**h** pan
9 laptop	**i** shelf
10 microwave	**j** cloth
11 table	**k** chair
12 towel	**l** rail
13 wash	**m** computer
14 washing	**n** heating
15 wastepaper	**o** basin

2 **In which room would you find each object?**

3 **Add a prefix from the box to make the words in the sentences negative.**

un dis in im

1 Penny is a very ......patient person. She doesn't like waiting for things.
2 I think the new school is very ......attractive compared to the lovely old buildings around it.
3 My pen has ......appeared. I can't find it anywhere.
4 ......fortunately, it's ......possible for me to come to your party on Saturday.
5 I'm afraid that my name has been spelled ......correctly.
6 David was ......able to give us a lift because his car has broken down.
7 One ......advantage of my new bag is that it has a rather short strap.

Grammar

4 **Choose the correct word(s).**

1 She's got some nice *furniture/furnitures* in her house.
2 I found some *information/informations* about flats to rent on a website.
3 She has long curly *hair/hairs* and wears glasses.
4 We had *spaghetti/spaghettis* for lunch.
5 Two black *coffee/coffees*, please.

Unit 5

Vocabulary

1 **How many words can you find in the wordsquare? Complete the sentences with the words you find.**

Across

1 If you drive to the airport, there is a large ...... near the terminal.
2 A ...... helps you to find your way in a new city.
3 The plane from Rome ...... at 12.00.
4 Because of bad weather, there are ...... of up to one hour on trains to London.
5 You have to carry a ...... when travelling in many foreign countries.
6 I'm sorry I'm late. The ...... on the motorway was terrible.
7 There's not a direct flight to Newcastle. You have to go ...... London.

Down

1 At the airport, you have to ...... your suitcase.
2 If you are meeting someone at the airport, you go to the ...... hall.
3 You can travel from Manchester to London by road, ... or air.
4 The ship leaves ...... at 7.00 tomorrow morning.
5 There is a bus ...... just opposite the hotel.
6 Which is the quickest ...... across the mountains?
7 You need to apply for a ...... if you want to visit certain countries.
8 After your plane lands, you have to collect your ....

C	A	R	P	A	R	K	L
H	R	A	O	X	O	V	U
E	R	I	R	S	U	V	G
C	I	L	T	T	T	I	G
K	V	I	A	O	E	S	A
I	A	M	A	P	W	A	G
N	L	A	N	D	S	K	E
Q	S	D	E	L	A	Y	S
P	A	S	S	P	O	R	T
T	R	A	F	F	I	C	Z

Grammar

2 **Complete the sentences with the correct prepositions.**

1 They decided to travel ...... road, rather than taking the train.
2 I hope that our flight arrives ...... time because my friend is waiting for me.
3 You are not allowed to take knives ...... the plane.
4 They checked ...... of the hotel and went home.
5 You have to wear a seatbelt while the plane is taking ...... and landing.
6 You have to book a seat on the coach ...... advance.
7 Children ...... to the age of 16 can travel at a reduced fare.
8 Cars have to ...... down when they pass through the city centre.

Unit 6

Vocabulary

1 Match the items (1–10) to the places where you can buy them (a–j).

1	magazine	**a**	gift shop
2	medicine	**b**	travel agent's
3	meat	**c**	baker's
4	bread	**d**	box office
5	souvenir	**e**	chemist's
6	petrol	**f**	post office
7	plane ticket	**g**	service station
8	stamp	**h**	garden centre
9	plant	**i**	newsagent's
10	theatre ticket	**j**	butcher's

2 Which of the items (1–10) could you also buy:

- on the Internet?
- in a supermarket?

3 Reorder the letters to make adjectives.

1	ritdy	......	**6**	ppayh	......
2	pemyt	......	**7**	nigrob	......
3	yonis	......	**8**	cixedet	......
4	saye	......	**9**	dure	......
5	chir	......	**10**	daxerel	......

4 Match the adjectives above to their opposites (a–j) below.

a	quiet	**f**	difficult
b	sad	**g**	poor
c	full	**h**	interesting
d	calm	**i**	polite
e	stressed	**j**	clean

Grammar

5 Complete the sentences with *some* or *any*.

1 Have you got ...... brothers or sisters?
2 Would you like ...... cake with your coffee?
3 There aren't ...... red peppers left, I'm afraid, only green ones.
4 Could you give me ...... information about computer games, please?
5 Have you seen ...... good films lately?
6 There isn't ...... milk in the fridge. Have we run out?
7 I'd like to buy ...... apples, please.
8 Would you like ...... black pepper on your pizza?

Unit 7

Vocabulary

1 Underline the word in each group which does not belong.

1 fry boil roast peel bake
2 cucumber melon orange sausage strawberry
3 bowl pastry pan cup dish
4 duck lamb steak turkey mushroom
5 soup lemonade onion juice milk
6 dessert snack picnic barbecue lunch

2 What is each person doing? Choose a word from the box.

apologising	warning	regretting	promising
agreeing	disagreeing	offering	
complaining	suggesting	refusing	

1 'I'm sorry I missed your party. I was ill.'
2 'I'll carry that bag for you if you like.'
3 'No thank you, I had one a few minutes ago.'
4 'I wish I hadn't said that Anne's hair looked funny.'
5 'You made a lot of noise last night. I couldn't get off to sleep.'
6 'I will remember to post your letter, honestly.'
7 'Why don't we go to the cinema this evening?'
8 'You're right – we should tell our parents where we're going.'
9 'Be careful. That water's very hot.'
10 'I'm sorry, but I don't think that's such a good idea.'

Grammar

3 Complete the gap in the second sentence using reported speech.

1 'Don't eat any more biscuits, Harry,' said his mother.
Harry's mother told him not .... biscuits.
2 'Boil the rice for forty minutes,' said the cookery teacher to her class.
The cookery teacher told her class .... for forty minutes.
3 'Don't burn the sauce, Diana,' said her father.
Diana's father told .... the sauce.
4 'Open the door for me please, Cathy,' said her sister.
Cathy's sister asked .... door.
5 'What are we having for dinner, Mum?' asked Tom.
Tom asked his mum what .... dinner.

Unit 8

Vocabulary

1 Reorder the words to make names of animals.

1	drib	......	**5**	bartib	......
2	gerti	......	**6**	meykon	......
3	derspi	......	**7**	toga	......
4	krash	......	**8**	noil	......

2 Write an adjective in each space by adding a suffix to the words in bold.

1 I like to see the ...... way of life in the places I visit. **tradition**
2 If you take that path up the mountain, you'll see a ...... waterfall. **wonder**
3 We spent a ...... afternoon relaxing by a lake. **please**
4 The best part of my trip was seeing the ...... scenery. **amaze**
5 There were a ...... number of tourists in such a remote area. **surprise**
6 I felt ...... when I tried to speak the local language. **embarrass**

Grammar

3 Choose the correct verb form.

1 I *am learning/learn* English at the moment.
2 I usually *am swimming/swim* in the sea in the summer.
3 We never *going/go* away on holiday because we have three dogs.
4 Do you *working/work* at the weekend?
5 Do you enjoy *reading/read* magazines?
6 Tammy *is getting/gets* up at seven o'clock every morning.
7 Connie *is having/has* a large wardrobe in her bedroom.
8 I don't like my bedroom *being/is* untidy.

Unit 9

Vocabulary

1 How many words can you find in the wordsquare? Complete the sentences with the words you find.

Across

1 ...... is the most popular water sport.
2 Athletes are trained by a ....
3 Going for a ...... around the park is a good way of keeping fit.
4 Table ...... is also known as *ping pong*.
5 Many simple games use a ...... and a ball.
6 To win at sport, you need a good level of ....
7 You wear ...... to move quickly over snow.

Down

1 Footballers usually wear a pair of ....
2 Playing ...... usually involves a long walk.
3 You wear a ...... for underwater sports.
4 ...... is a team game played on a frozen surface.
5 ...... is a type of football that uses an oval ball.
6 You have to get the ball over a ...... in volleyball.
7 ...... involves hitting a ball against a wall.
8 The winner of a race usually wins a ....
9 To win a football match, a team must score at least one ....
10 Most athletes wear a ...... when they're training.

S	W	I	M	M	I	N	G	T
H	E	C	O	A	C	H	P	R
O	T	E	N	N	I	S	R	A
R	S	H	R	U	N	Q	I	C
T	U	O	U	K	E	U	Z	K
S	I	C	G	J	T	A	E	S
G	T	K	B	A	T	S	G	U
O	N	E	Y	X	J	H	O	I
L	N	Y	S	K	I	S	A	T
F	I	T	N	E	S	S	L	J

2 Match (1–10) to (a–h) to make the names of health problems. Some words in a–h can be used more than once.

1	head	**a**	throat
2	sore	**b**	arm
3	broken	**c**	ache
4	high	**d**	finger
5	cut	**e**	sick
6	ear	**f**	ankle
7	tooth	**g**	nose
8	feel	**h**	temperature
9	twisted		
10	runny		

Grammar

3 Complete the sentences with *if* or *unless*.

1 I don't go out ...... I've finished my homework.
2 ...... you lend me your new CD, I'll help you with your maths.
3 I won't go out ...... it stops raining because I don't want to get wet.
4 You shouldn't play sports ...... you have a temperature.
5 ...... you train hard, you can't hope to become a top sportsperson.
6 ...... we're lucky, we should arrive just in time to see the match.

Unit 10

Vocabulary

1 Write a noun in each space by adding a suffix to the words in bold.

1 I went to see an ...... of modern art. **exhibit**
2 I think there are too many ...... on television. **advertise**
3 The price for ...... to the theme park is quite high. **admit**
4 Have you got an Internet ...... in your hotel room? **connect**
5 I'm going to see the latest film by my favourite .... **direct**
6 I think e-mail is the easiest form of .... **communicate**
7 We have quite a lot of electrical ...... in our classroom. **equip**
8 The singer gave an excellent ...... at the concert. **perform**

Grammar

2 Complete the sentences with the correct words.

1 I think that text messaging is more fun ...... e-mailing.
2 I prefer watching a DVD ...... going to the cinema.
3 Who does this Mp3 player belong ...... ?
4 If I were you, I'd get a more ...... to date computer.
5 I ...... afford to buy a new printer until next month.
6 Tony is borrowing a digital camera ...... his brother.
7 I ...... a headache if I look at a screen for too long.
8 It was ...... a cold evening that they decided to stay in and watch television.

Irregular verbs

present	past simple	past participle
be	was/were	been
beat	beat	beaten
become	became	become
begin	began	begun
bend	bent	bent
bite	bit	bitten
bleed	bled	bled
blow	blew	blown
break	broke	broken
bring	brought	brought
build	built	built
burn	burnt	burnt
buy	bought	bought
catch	caught	caught
choose	chose	chosen
come	came	come
cost	cost	cost
cut	cut	cut
dig	dug	dug
do	did	done
draw	drew	drawn
dream	dreamt	dreamt
drink	drank	drunk
drive	drove	driven
eat	ate	eaten
fall	fell	fallen
feed	fed	fed
feel	felt	felt
fight	fought	fought
find	found	found
fly	flew	flown
forget	forgot	forgotten
forgive	forgave	forgiven
freeze	froze	frozen
get	got	got
give	gave	given
go	went	gone
grow	grew	grown
have	had	had
hear	heard	heard
hide	hid	hidden
hit	hit	hit
hold	held	held
hurt	hurt	hurt
keep	kept	kept
know	knew	known
lay	laid	laid
lead	led	led

present	past simple	past participle
learn	learnt	learnt
leave	left	left
lend	lent	lent
let	let	let
lie	lay	lain
light	lit	lit
lose	lost	lost
make	made	made
mean	meant	meant
meet	met	met
pay	paid	paid
put	put	put
read	read	read
ride	rode	ridden
ring	rang	rung
rise	rose	risen
run	ran	run
say	said	said
see	saw	seen
sell	sold	sold
send	sent	sent
set	set	set
shake	shook	shaken
shine	shone	shone
shoot	shot	shot
show	showed	shown
shut	shut	shut
sing	sang	sung
sit	sat	sat
sleep	slept	slept
smell	smelt	smelt
speak	spoke	spoken
spell	spelt	spelt
spend	spent	spent
spread	spread	spread
stand	stood	stood
steal	stole	stolen
sweep	swept	swept
swim	swam	swum
take	took	taken
teach	taught	taught
tear	tore	torn
tell	told	told
think	thought	thought
throw	threw	thrown
wake	woke	woken
wear	wore	worn
win	won	won
write	wrote	written